BREAKING *AWAY*
FROM THE
PACK

JON RAMBEAU

BREAKING

AWAY

FROM THE
PACK

How to Spend Your Career Currency to Work Smarter,
Move Faster, and Reach the Top!

Advantage.

Published by Advantage, Charleston, South Carolina.
Member of Advantage Media Group.

ADVANTAGE is a registered trademark, and the Advantage colophon is a trademark of Advantage Media Group, Inc.

Printed in the United States of America.

10 9 8 7 6 5 4 3 2 1

ISBN: 978-1-64225-135-7
LCCN: 2019915818

Cover design by Mary Hamilton.
Layout design by Megan Elger.

This publication is designed to provide accurate and authoritative information in regard to the subject matter covered. It is sold with the understanding that the publisher is not engaged in rendering legal, accounting, or other professional services. If legal advice or other expert assistance is required, the services of a competent professional person should be sought.

Advantage Media Group is proud to be a part of the Tree Neutral® program. Tree Neutral offsets the number of trees consumed in the production and printing of this book by taking proactive steps such as planting trees in direct proportion to the number of trees used to print books. To learn more about Tree Neutral, please visit www.treeneutral.com.

Advantage Media Group is a publisher of business, self-improvement, and professional development books and online learning. We help entrepreneurs, business leaders, and professionals share their Stories, Passion, and Knowledge to help others Learn & Grow. Do you have a manuscript or book idea that you would like us to consider for publishing? Please visit advantagefamily.com or call 1.866.775.1696.

CONTENTS

PART III: LESSONS I'VE LEARNED

PREFACE

The plane had climbed through ten thousand feet, lifting through the thin blanket of clouds above the city. I was pulling my laptop out of my bag when my colleague asked a seemingly innocuous question.

"You seem pretty passionate about career and leadership," she said. "Have you ever considered writing a book?"

We were on the back end of a long travel day that, for me, had included speaking to hundreds of future Lockheed Martin leaders about launching their careers. It was a talk I had given dozens of times to thousands of young employees and have given many times since. The topic never fails to bring my energy level to a crescendo.

As I sat beside my colleague on the airplane, there was a long pause. Then, I reluctantly pulled the tattered, yellow pages out of my bag, where I had kept them for years. I'd been thinking about this book for at least a decade—and never told a soul.

Twenty years earlier, I had joined Lockheed Martin straight out of college. I'd moved quickly in my career. By age thirty-six, I'd become a corporate vice president—one of the youngest VPs in company history. A few years later, I was named one of the Top 40 Under 40 executives in the aerospace and defense industry by

Aviation Week & Space Technology. All the while, I quietly collected themes and stories. Recorded anecdotes. Built an outline from the experiences I had and the things I learned. But I had never really gotten serious about putting pen to paper, or fingers to keyboard.

As my colleague flipped through the pages, I held my breath. Finally, she looked up at me.

"This is really good, Jon. I think you have something here."

"Really?"

"Really."

While that conversation came and went in a heartbeat, it helped provide the encouragement I needed to dust off those ragged pages and crack open the Mac.

It has taken three years of plane rides and stolen weekend nights—all while running a large, growing business within my company and working hard to be the best dad I can to two amazing girls—but I've finally gotten this one up off the runway.

This book is based on my journey, my experiences, and my observations. I sincerely hope it will be helpful to you as you strive to accelerate your professional success and break away from the pack in ways only you can define.

I can buy anything I want, basically, but I can't buy time.

—WARREN BUFFETT

INTRODUCTION

WHAT IS CAREER CURRENCY?

Every year in the US, millions of college graduates enter the professional workforce. The job market they are entering includes fewer than 2.5 million management positions, most of them occupied.

There are fewer than 200,000 US jobs that hold the title *chief executive*. That may seem like a large number, but consider the fact that of the chief executive positions, less than 3,700 of them lead a publicly traded company, and this number has steadily declined since the late 1990s. At large companies, CEO turnover averages approximately 13 percent each year, which would suggest about 25,000 chief executive roles opening annually in the US. Fewer than 500 of those would be with publicly traded firms.

Think about those statistics.

There are millions of professionals entering the workforce each year, and those who aim to reach the top will face fierce competition. There will be room at the top for just a very fortunate few. If these proportions stay consistent, about 0.5 percent of graduates today can hope to obtain a top executive position in the future. To lead a publicly traded firm, that number drops to about 0.01 percent.

But reaching a top executive position may not be the measure of success in your chosen field. In today's workforce, there are many paths to the top of one's profession, and career milestones may be highly individualized. It is estimated, for example, that in 2017, the number of freelancers reached 57.3 million—a surprising 36 percent of the total US workforce. If you're entering the world of freelancing, reaching the top may be described in different ways: by amassing a number of stable, high-paying contracts with well-regarded institutions; or by commanding a significant hourly premium over others in your field.

Whatever your chosen profession—and however precisely "the top" is defined within that field—if you're early in your career and seek to rise quickly through the ranks, this book is for you. This book is for you if your career is already underway and you are not pleased with your path or progression. This is for you if you want to truly excel and to advance faster than your peers. This book is *not* for those who desire moderate success but rather for those who wish to be professionally *exceptional*.

What does it mean to be professionally exceptional? In many ways, this is up to you. From my perspective, it means reaching your most ambitious professional goal. It means getting there rapidly, and in a way that allows you to maintain some level of balance and harmony in your life. It means navigating your way without expending unnecessary effort. It means working hard and working smart. It means finding happiness and satisfaction when you get there.

While this book will describe many keys to success, it centers on the one ingredient every professional brings to their career journey in roughly equal measure: *time*. Time is a career currency that is issued to each of us in finite quantity. On average, we are all granted roughly the same number of days, weeks, months, and years to spend as we see fit. How we allocate that time across the different dimensions of our lives, and where we focus the portion we dedicate to our careers, is of huge importance.

In the pages ahead, you will learn how to spend your limited career currency wisely, focusing your energy on early and rapid career advancement and limiting unnecessary expenditures—in essence, getting it right the first time. As you will see, those who spend wisely in their early career will have a much better probability of reaching positions of great responsibility. This early success—*Breaking Away from the Pack*—will be essential to getting ahead, and perhaps going all the way to the top!

HOW DO I USE THIS BOOK?

One of the most important communication lessons I have learned as an executive is *know your audience.* This advice is easy to follow when speaking to a defined group of people. It becomes much more challenging when writing a book that could be picked up by almost anyone. Nonetheless, I have given some thought to the question of how this book can be most useful to a very broad and diverse audience.

When I purchase a business book, I sometimes feel guilty jumping to the sections that most interest me, fearing that I might not get the full value the author intended. If I'm honest with myself, I believe there is also some feeling of implied obligation to the author to ensure I digest their full work exactly as they had intended. For those who may suffer from similar afflictions, allow me to put your mind at ease. For many readers, the best use of this book will be to jump around, revisit, or even skip completely certain sections of the book—you have my permission!

Those who are my age or older may remember a series of children's books called Choose Your Own Adventure. At the end of each section the reader was given a choice to make and, based on that choice, was directed to a different page to continue their individualized journey. I recommend the reader adopt a similar philosophy to using this book, based on where you are in your professional journey.

The key to getting the most out of *Breaking Away from the Pack* will be to match your individual circumstances with your use of the book. Each of the three parts serves a different purpose and will be useful at different points in your career. Along with the advice offered in each part, I have included watch areas called "Taxes and Tariffs" to highlight pitfalls to be avoided because they will erode your career currency—significantly in some cases. Even if you are skipping a whole part of the book, I recommend reviewing these at a minimum.

If you are just beginning your career and charting your course from scratch, I would highly recommend reading the entire book front to back, with a strong focus on working through the exercises suggested in part I, "Assessment, Planning, and Positioning." I have also made templates for some of the exercises available for download at www.jonrambeau.com. As your career progresses, the second and especially third parts ("Taking Action" and "Lessons I've Learned") should become reference material to be reviewed again in the future as needed when you encounter specific challenges and opportunities along your journey.

If you are an experienced professional looking for redirection or acceleration of a career, I certainly recommend a review of part I. While this part of the book will be of great utility to recent college graduates, it may not be as useful to all seasoned professionals. If upon a cursory review you feel you have a thorough understanding of self and a strong sense of your desired career path, it may make the most sense to move to a deeper reading of parts II and III.

If you are already moving along well in your professional journey and are pleased with your progress, this book may serve you best as a further accelerator, with part III being your best area for focused reading and occasional reference as you encounter professional challenges.

If your circumstances don't quite fit any of the scenarios above, I recommend you start by reviewing the introduction to each of the three parts, and from there, Choose Your Own Adventure.

PART I

ASSESSMENT, PLANNING, AND POSITIONING

Stephen Covey's book *The 7 Habits of Highly Effective People* is widely regarded as one of the best business books of all time. The second habit he discusses is "Begin With the End in Mind." While in the context of Covey's book this advice is directed more toward our life's end and a more holistic consideration of what matters, the same thought process applies to your career. If professional success is an important cornerstone of your life's story, it warrants some thoughtful consideration.

Time is our most valued career currency, and it should be spent wisely. Given that we spend this currency every day whether we like it or not, most aspiring professionals will be eager to jump right in and get started wherever the best opportunity presents itself. But we would all be wise to heed Covey's advice and first consider the end.

What are our professional goals and aspirations, and how can we best get there?

While a "jump right in" mentality might maximize the immediate use of time and yield early results, it could ultimately lead to months, or even years, of career currency spent moving up the wrong professional ladder. The key to avoiding this outcome is thoughtful, up-front analysis and planning.

Taking a few days, weeks, or even months prior to launching or repositioning your career can yield significant dividends over time.

This first part of the book outlines the planning necessary to pair you with the best career path—the one that will fully leverage your strengths and experience while also increasing your probability of personal and professional satisfaction.

Understanding yourself is important. Equally important is understanding the industry and the company you work in or are considering working in. In the first three chapters, you will learn how to do exactly that, and how to leverage this understanding to best position yourself for exceptional results.

CHAPTER 1

KNOW THYSELF

Understand Your Strengths—and Your Passions

The first step in building an exceptional career is a fundamental understanding of self, looking across the various dimensions of our talents, strengths, and personal preferences. At the heart of this understanding is a very important intersection of two questions:

- What do you enjoy?

- What are you good at?

While there are many layers to understanding ourselves, the intersection of these two fundamental questions is generally where we will find both personal satisfaction and professional success. Applying this understanding of self to your career planning will maximize the value of your career currency spent, increasing the odds that you will find your targeted career to be both enjoyable and rewarding.

To truly understand ourselves, we must start by being honest. In establishing our own vision of success, it's important to filter out impressions of what the world around us considers "successful" as well as the expectations set by friends, family, and colleagues.

Take my situation, for example. As a young boy, I always wanted to be a doctor. Why is that? Well, through sixth grade, I attended a small private school. While my mother was a teacher there, and I consequently received a significant tuition benefit, the majority of my classmates came from wealthy families. The school was across town in an affluent neighborhood, and there was a large medical center nearby. Combine these factors and you can easily understand the prevailing situation in the school—in each class, a disproportionate percentage of students had physician parents.

Growing up in this environment, I observed the affluence and lifestyle afforded my classmates, and I heard over and over about their parents' successes. Some of the parents were, in fact, world-renowned physicians at the top of their profession. It should come as no surprise that, over time, I equated success with being a doctor.

Looking back, I can easily imagine myself holding on to this view of success and pursuing it. Could I have studied to become a doctor? Of course. Could I have succeeded? Probably. But would I have enjoyed it? Would it have played to my natural abilities?

In retrospect, I see several elements that most likely would have resulted in my being a mediocre doctor at best.

First, medicine isn't an area in which I have any special talents. The best doctors are noted for their high degree of empathy and patience. They're able to function well while surrounded by the extremes of human suffering and deal with people calmly under these circumstances. While I could likely have developed these skills (and indeed, some of them are required of me today), they would not have come naturally to me early in my career. I was very focused and driven as a young adult. Patience was not a virtue for me, and as a strongly analytical introvert, I don't think I would have had the best bedside manner either.

Second—and more to the point—I don't believe I would have enjoyed the work. I've known many doctors personally, and I know how they're required to spend their time. There are long days of surgery punctuated by long days of office appointments and, at senior levels, a healthy dose of administrative responsibility to boot. Many doctors I know tell me that the more successful they become, the more time they have to spend doing things other than tending to their patients, which is exactly what many of them were most passionate about when they started their careers.

As a young child looking forward, it was easy to focus on the academic and professional prestige as well as the financial rewards of this career path. Fortunately, as I grew older, I developed a better understanding of self that led me in a different professional direction—and away from a career where I probably would have risen only to mediocrity.

You might now be wondering how you can develop this understanding of self. Certainly free-form self-reflection may be effective for some people, and there may be a few out there who already have great conviction about their personal strengths and career prospects, and how the two intersect. But I strongly encourage the use of a more structured process to think this through. There are two primary elements of self that I recommend you consider. These are *what you are good at* and *what will make you happy*.

ASSESSING WHAT YOU'RE GOOD AT

Of the two assessment areas, this one is where you will find a breadth of tools available to assist you. There are many strengths and skills assessment instruments available to you, and I want to outline a few as a starting point. However, you should not limit yourself to these—I encourage you to cast a wide net and explore the range of instruments available for self-assessment and reflection.

Myers-Briggs Type Indicator (MBTI)

The MBTI instrument is a tried-and-true gauge of personality type. I recall that when I completed this self-evaluation in my first year out of college, I learned that my type was INTJ. This personality type suggests success in "creating business plans, implementing campaigns, and reaching strategic goals." Clearly, this was a factor in leading me to believe that I was suited for executive roles in the future.

You can access several versions of tests that use the Myers-Briggs approach exclusively or in tandem with other methodologies. The most trusted and popular version is the official MBTI instrument from the Myers & Briggs Foundation, found at https://www.myers-briggs.org.

NERIS Type Explorer

Similar to the MBTI in its use of four-letter initialisms to depict personalities, the NERIS is distinct in methodology. While Myers-Briggs tests make use of personality theories suggested by psychologist Carl Jung, NERIS incorporates "the Big Five personality traits, a model that dominates modern psychological and social research."

Requiring an average of twelve minutes or less to complete, the test results include a detailed section on career choices. You can take the NERIS free at the website https://www.16personalities.com.

Keirsey Temperament Sorter

This is a tool specifically designed to assist professionals in evaluating career options and weighing those options against their innate strengths and preferences. The tool focuses on four temperament types (artisan, guardian, idealist, and rational) and provides a report that suggests careers with which you may be most compatible. Learn more at https://www.keirsey.com.

Fascination Advantage

This is an instrument I experimented with later in my career and found quite interesting. It provides a slight twist on the MBTI, focusing on how the world sees you and thus what your strengths are through someone else's eyes. This instrument highlights your personal strengths and offers guidance on how to leverage those professionally to be even stronger. It's a great resource to aid you in thinking through your personal compatibility with a range of career options. You can take the test free at https://www.howtofascinate.com.

The MAPP Career Assessment

Short for Motivational Appraisal Personal Potential, the MAPP test includes seventy-one questions, which test-takers are encouraged to answer quickly so the answers are reflexive. The MAPP assessment includes a job-matching service for interested individuals and offers both free and paid versions. Detailed information and the test itself are available at https://www.assessment.com.

Self-Directed Search

Finally, you might consider the Self-Directed Search, also known as the SDS, which is based on the theories of renowned psychologist John Holland. This test, which takes about twenty minutes to complete, asks questions about your "aspirations, activities, competencies, interests, and other self-estimates" to match you with the type of work environment ideally suited to your personality.

Heavily focused on career paths, the SDS provides a report that includes suggestions for career and study areas associated with your personality type, information about jobs associated with your "daydream occupations," salary data about your recommended fields, and links to related career resources. You can access the test at http://www.self-directed-search.com.

The resources above represent only a short list of personality tests that may be useful for defining, refining, and validating what you're good at as well as the roles you're best suited for. Again, I encourage you to cast a wide net to explore this important element of self. Whatever time and effort you devote to getting a better grasp on your suitability for certain careers is an investment of time that will pay a dividend of career currency—helping you to avoid costly errors and start spending wisely from day one.

TAXES AND TARIFFS: TO LEAD OR NOT TO LEAD?

One of the most pivotal decisions of any career is whether or not you will choose to lead people. And unfortunately, this is one of the decisions many people take much more lightly than they should. I find most people I work with who are early in their careers tend to equate success with leading large organizations, and while this is one measure of success, there are other paths that do not involve leading people. For example, from the introduction you may recall that over a third of the US workforce is comprised of freelance employees. This group would include consultants and other highly specialized employees for hire. There will be many highly successful professionals in this group, and as a general rule, a freelance employee will not be managing a large organization.

The critical difference here that many people overlook is the one between individual results and team results. If you choose to lead people, your results—and therefore your long-term success—will depend on the performance of your team. If you choose not to lead people, your success will be linked much more closely to your individual capabilities and accomplishments. As you assess your strengths, be honest with yourself about your ability and desire to lead people. It is challenging. It can be rewarding. And it is not for everyone. It requires different skills and is a very different experience. Before you head down this path, be sure it is for you.

ASSESSING WHAT MAKES YOU HAPPY

This is the part of self-assessment that is, by definition, more "free-form." I would suggest first answering a set of broad questions regarding your preferences and interests and then using your answers as a filter for the range of careers, companies, and industries you are considering. A useful list might include the following questions to ask yourself:

- What geographic areas appeal to me most? Is it a priority to remain close to my hometown and family? What kind of climate do I prefer? Does a big-city or small-town experience appeal to me more?

- What cultures appeal to me? Which do not?

- What products, technologies, and markets appeal to me?

- Are there certain ethical or moral causes that I wish to pursue?

- Do I want the opportunity to travel frequently, or do I prefer more downtime at home?

- Do I value stability over flexibility or vice versa?

- Would I enjoy steadily working my way up through an existing corporate structure, or would I like the idea of being in charge as soon as possible—even if it entails risk?

- Would I be happiest pursuing my own ideas (possibly as part of a startup)?

- How do I feel when the pressure is on? Do I thrive in these intense scenarios, or do I perform best when I have a consistent, predictable workload as well as a timeline for task completion?

- Do I need regular social contact with others throughout the day, or do I perform best in a more solitary environment?

Whether you work with this list of questions or choose to formulate your own, spend some focused time thinking through them honestly. Consider what will really work for you and where you will find happiness. Try not to let the expectations of people around you creep in. This needs to be about you, because without personal happiness, it will be very difficult to ever make others happy. As you work through your thought process, keep notes on the questions you considered and how you feel about each of them.

REDIRECTION

There are two additional scenarios that are important to consider if you are already pursuing a career: finding you are either (1) not as good at it, or (2) not as happy with it as you had initially anticipated. In these scenarios, it might be best to consider either a *course correction* or a *pivot*. While you may not wish to spend the time necessary to make a change, it is critical that you be honest with yourself about the trade-off of career currency versus your long-term success and personal satisfaction. Let's explore each of these redirection options by looking at a couple of examples.

COURSE CORRECTIONS

A course correction is a relatively minor adjustment to your career trajectory. As I would define it, it involves changing one, or at most two, dimensions of your professional direction. This may mean you decide to pursue a career with a different company, doing similar work to what you have been doing. It may mean you stay within the same company but take on responsibilities that are better suited to your strengths. It may mean you simply transfer to a different department to work under better leadership.

Regardless of what dimension you change, course corrections generally do not involve a wholesale repositioning of your career path, consume a lot of your career currency, or involve a tremendous amount of risk.

In my early days as a leader, I managed a small portfolio of contracts focused on IT and security systems. A bright young man named James, the project manager for a small IT services contract, worked for me at the time. His employees liked him, and he seemed to enjoy his work. In fact, he spoke often of his aspirations to rise through the project management field to reach levels of director and beyond.

As I continued to work with James, however, I observed some areas of concern. First, his attention to detail was lacking. He also relied heavily on personal relationships and a hefty dose of delegation to get his job done. Consequently, the performance of his projects was inconsistent. To his customers, however, his personal energy and charisma more than offset these shortcomings.

While James could probably have continued on the project management career path and enjoyed it, he was never going to be truly exceptional given his natural orientation. When I had worked with James for about a year, I suggested that he may want to consider taking an assignment in our business development organization, where he could better leverage his strengths.

His initial reaction was lukewarm. While he realized his strengths may be better leveraged there, he had become convinced that "success" equaled advancement in project management. Just as I had convinced myself as a young child that success meant being a doctor, he had become determined that professional success meant rising through the project management organization to pursue a general management role.

Eventually, I convinced James to try the business development role on a trial basis. It became quickly apparent this was where his natural abilities lie, and he realized that he enjoyed the role immensely! The rest is history. Today, he is a highly regarded international marketing professional within our company, living with his family overseas. While it took a bit of career refocusing, he has flourished professionally since this course correction and—from all evidence—has found great personal satisfaction.

This is just one example of someone who had the courage to challenge their vision for professional success and rethink their path to the top. It is important to recognize the need to do this and to take action rather than continue to expend career currency toward an objective for which you are not well suited.

PIVOTS

Pivots are a different animal altogether. Pivots, as I define them, are significant professional shifts involving change across many dimensions of your professional (and often personal) life. They can be daunting, challenging, and complex. So much so that books have been dedicated to them. One of these, by Jenny Blake, is actually titled *Pivot* and provides a blueprint for navigating these monumental life decisions. While I'm sure there are other resources to draw upon when considering a pivot, I recommend Blake's book because it aligns very well with my philosophy of considering where your capabilities and happiness intersect to find true professional satisfaction.

Now, let's consider what a pivot might look like.

Prior to my time working with James, I managed a regional effort to upgrade airport security systems. While in this capacity, I had the chance to work with Julie, a talented project manager—the best on my team. Julie managed her resources efficiently, and she surprised me one day when she called to say, "I don't think I really need the team of four you've given me to run this project. Can I send two of them back?" It was somewhat unheard of to voluntarily give up team members when working on a large project.

The better I got to know Julie, the more impressed I became with her consistent results, attention to detail, and bottom-line financial returns. While she seemed to enjoy her work, there were a few occasions when she talked about her hobbies and interests. Cooking came up time and again. She wished she had more time for it, and being on the road so often left her with very little.

After I was reassigned, I kept tabs on Julie here and there over the next several years. At one point I learned she had moved on to manage a larger project with more responsibility. She continued to excel, and I had no doubt she would rise to the top someday.

A few years later, I needed someone like Julie and sought her out. To my surprise, she had left the company. Wanting to understand her decision better, I tracked down her last manager and asked what had happened. Apparently, Julie had arrived at the office one day and resigned. Why? She had decided project management was not for her. Her passion had always been to be a chef, and she had decided to pursue that life ambition. Because he'd kept in touch with her, that manager knew that Julie had opened her own restaurant. Little to my surprise, it was a smashing success. Julie was truly happy.

A pivot like Julie's takes staggering courage, but this courage is sometimes necessary if you are to be true to yourself.

If you are already invested to some degree in a particular career path and suspect you may need a course correction or pivot, I encourage you to follow the steps previously outlined in this chapter to ensure you revector in the right direction and maximize the value of your remaining career currency.

EXERCISE: BRINGING IT TOGETHER

Once you have worked through an assessment of your strengths, considered where you might find happiness, and evaluated any need for redirection, I suggest creating a simple matrix to compare and contrast the range of career paths, companies, and/or industries you are considering. You may use the sample format I offer on the following page or formulate your own. If you use my format, complete the matrix for each of the career paths you are evaluating. Evaluating the range of options you are considering will provide an objective look at what may be the top two to three career paths that will set you up for extraordinary success and long-term happiness. What's most important is to be true to who you are and to develop a foundational understanding of self that will best position you to be in control of your career currency and spend it wisely from the start.

Career Path Evaluation: Tech Startup CTO

Top Skills Required for Success (10 or Less)	Importance (1-5)	My Proficiency (1-5)	Total Score
1. Advanced technical degree and deep technical expertise	5	4	20
2. Ability to lead diverse teams in an unstructured environment	4	3	12
3. Ability to market company products and capabilities to customers and investors	3	5	15
4. Ability to anticipate and adjust to rapidly changing market conditions	4	3	12
Sum of "Importance" and "Total Score"	16		59
Proficiency Score (Divide Total Score by Importance)			3.7

Career Attributes and Their Importance to Me (10 or Less)	Importance to Me (1-5)	Career Has This Attribute (1-5)	Total Score
1. Job Security and Predictability	1	1	1
2. Potential for Substantial Reward	5	5	25
3. Reasonable stress level	2	2	4
4. Regular work schedule; good quality of life outside of work	2	1	2
5. Reasonable cost of living	3	2	6
Sum of "Importance" and "Total Score"	13		38
Attribute Compatibility Score (Divide Total Score by Importance to Me)			2.9
Proficiency Score (I will be "Good At" this)			**3.7**
Attribute Compatibility Score (I will "Enjoy" this)			**2.9**

For those who are analytical thinkers, this template may be useful as an objective way to contrast your compatibility with different career paths by assigning a numerical score. Complete one for each career path you are considering. Download an electronic version at www.jonrambeau.com.

CHAPTER 2

ASK WHAT WORKS

Map the Path to Your Objective

I walked through the door of Lockheed Martin straight out of college and began working in quality assurance. While the role provided me some valuable experience, I realized—quickly—that QA was not where I wanted to spend my career. Fortunately, I was also part of the company's leadership development program, and as a participant in that program I had completed assessment and planning exercises like the ones described in chapter 1. Undertaking some thoughtful self-assessment and reflection helped me realize that what I really wanted was to gain experience and develop my skills in program management and to ultimately become a general manager for a business unit. The planning exercise also prepared me for the fact that it would take time—and some targeted career moves—to get there.

Through the leadership development program, I undertook a series of assignments in our operations organization, all the while pursuing a master's degree and taking on special assignments that would prepare me for program management assignments. After completing my master's degree, I made my first significant step forward with a move to Washington, DC, where I took on a rotational assignment supporting one of our division presidents in a role that was similar to a chief of staff. I worked closely with the boss to ensure he had what he needed each day, and I traveled with him wherever he went. This represented a transition geographically as well as from one type of role to one entirely different. While the geographic move was exciting, it was the latter that really excited me—an opportunity to begin learning what it really takes to run a business.

The role supporting a division president was a pivotal role that vectored me toward a series of increasingly responsible program management and program director positions. After working my way through several similar roles with increasing responsibility, I received an exciting assignment as a corporate vice president. With this came another geographic transfer and another promotion. In addition to deepening my experience in engineering and technology, it allowed me an opportunity to work directly for a member of our CEO's leadership team. There was significant education to be gained in this role, and it substantially broadened my experience in the advanced technology domain.

My next two moves left the biggest impact on my career. The first saw me going to work in our aircraft division on a large multinational fighter aircraft program. For the next few years, I led the international portion of that project. I gained invaluable experience in the field of military aviation as well as international business.

In the second of these moves, I assumed my first general management position—leading a business unit for our corporation. This has incrementally led to my leadership of businesses with greater complexity and revenue to the role I have today.

Lockheed Martin is an exciting company to work for. It is large, not only in terms of staff and annual revenue but also variety. We manufacture an impressive array of products across a broad domestic and international footprint. There are a multitude of career paths to be pursued and developed, and in many cases one can lead to another based on intersectionality of geography, product domain, or leadership chain.

I've shared the preceding details—which hit only the highlights—to show how, even within a single company, I was able to map out my path, obtain the knowledge and experience I knew I needed, and incrementally move toward a role that perfectly aligned with the goals I set at the very beginning. In other words—I feel good about my investment of career currency.

THE RIGHT PATH FOR WHERE YOU WANT TO GO

In today's professional world, it's well known that the majority of people do not hire into a company and stay for the duration of their career. The same expectation was set for me when I joined the workforce in the mid-1990s: *You won't stay at a company longer than five years.* While my path turned out to be an exception, the standard rule does hold true for many people.

What applies to most of us, whether we move from company to company or just between departments within a single organization, is that we generally stick to one *field*. And within every field, there's a path to the top—a path that may not be obvious from the outside looking in but tends to be defined, consistent, and (most importantly) learnable.

Take, for instance, the aerospace and defense industry. The route to the top tends to wind through the technical and project management disciplines. For computer engineers and systems analysts, ultimate long-term success is often marked by a focus on consulting work. Meanwhile, the career trajectory from retail banker to banking executive involves team management, often starting at the team leader level and progressing through single-location and regional management positions.

We often assume we already know what types of experience and knowledge we need. In many industries, the formula for reaching the top *seems* evident. But even in these cases (perhaps especially in these cases), it's very important that we do our homework. We have to find out which specific—often less obvious—experiences mark the difference between moderate and exceptional success.

Consider venture capital. Hiring at these firms is intensely competitive. It's a field in which making it through the door is, in itself, a major milestone and as such requires recruits to have already amassed the right experience and made smart career moves. This is also a field where the desirable credentials may be less obvious than they appear. In an interview with Glassdoor, Charles Hudson, managing partner at a VC firm, explains that the two main things that help would-be venture capitalists succeed are (1) having served for a long period of time on the board of a very successful company (long enough that the company's success can be linked to your contributions), and (2) expertise in a "hot" investment sector (the technology realm certainly qualifies, though it's a moving target that would-be VCs need to monitor continuously).

Regardless of where you plan to work, it's important to understand the norms for advancement—the experiences that are necessary in that company or line of work if you want to realize your professional objectives. The next question, then, is *how*. If common perceptions regarding the steps to success across industries are frequently wrong or at a minimum unclear, it stands to reason that there's plenty of misinformation out there. This is one area of many in which having a mentor is invaluable.

DON'T GO DOWN THE PATH WITHOUT A GUIDE

In 2006, I was advised by one of our division presidents that experience in our aircraft division would be a significant career enhancer for me. Why? Because this would be a core segment of our business with great professional growth potential for decades to come. Experience in this area would open many professional doors and offer a unique experience that would serve me well as I advanced to more senior levels. I had no aviation knowledge and no relationships in that part of our company. But I placed this experience on my list of career objectives.

In 2010, a former mentor of mine transitioned into a key leadership role in this division. I contacted him and began a dialogue. After about six months, a position opened up and he called me. I accepted immediately over the phone because I knew this was an essential career stepping stone for me.

This important example underscores the value of actively seeking advice from those with deep knowledge of your industry or your company. And it introduces one of the most important topics we'll cover in this book: mentors.

SENIOR EXECUTIVE EXPOSURE AND SUPPORT

We will explore the topic of mentoring more broadly in chapter 6. However, it's worth mentioning here how pivotal your relationship with mentors is to accomplishing your goals. An engaged mentor can help orient you to the organization you're working within and provide counsel—counsel that comes from a place of firsthand experience and trial and error—on how to get from where you are to where you want to be.

When you sit down to talk with a mentor, your first order of business should be making it clear where you are now and where you want to be. There will be time for more detailed discussions later. Down the road, you can delve into specific skills, day-to-day problem resolution, and the tactics of getting your job done well. You'll have your chance to explain how you're not getting along with Steve or Deborah and to receive sound advice on interpersonal office relationships. But before you get into strategy or real-time issues, your mentor needs to understand these two things: *where you are* and *where you want to be.*

It was a mentoring conversation I had with one of my advisors a long time ago that brought the importance of industry-specific career paths into sharp focus for me. This advisor told me that every company had a path to the top. In my company, that path could involve either strong technical leadership—leading to business leadership positions—or a strong skill set in program management. While there were other paths, these would be the best for me to reach my goals in my company. In other companies, he pointed out, the path might be through the marketing organization, through sales, through research and development, or a myriad of other disciplines.

This mentor put the thought in my head that every company has, essentially, a formula for success in a given field. After our conversation, I paid more attention, and I noticed how true this was. I could see that the top executives in most companies tended to come from one or two particular disciplines or to have common experiences—and that these backgrounds varied from industry to industry and company to company.

The method most people are a taught for planning their career boils down to stating, "Well, I'll do this today. In ten or fifteen years, I want to be doing that." Then they are taught to look at new opportunities as they arise and make sensible comparisons on factors that usually include income, lifestyle, professional satisfaction, and degree of career advancement. The missing link I usually see is the lack of a long-term experience framework through which to evaluate each incremental move. In essence, I see people evaluating the short-term benefit of a move at the expense of understanding the long-term impact on their ultimate career goals.

Now that I often serve in the mentor's role, I regularly discuss this very matter with those who turn to me for advice. For instance, I recently met with a mentee from our communications organization. In her current role, she writes press releases, handles media engagements, develops communications strategies, and leads teams of communications professionals. She called me to discuss the merits of pursuing an alternate career path in program management, and I was very honest with her.

"At the level where you are now," I explained, "it will be very difficult to secure a program management position at the same level. Without demonstrating successful program management at lower levels in the organization, you will have a hard time competing for the more senior roles."

What I did with this employee—honestly addressing the limitations of prior experience within a new field—is a critical dimension of mentorship. A mentor who has the right perspective can help you avoid pursuing an unsuccessful strategy and can also redirect you toward paths that extend, naturally and predictably, from where you are now. While I did tell my mentee that program management may not be the best investment of her career currency, I also endorsed a different pursuit. The skills she had honed in her communications role made her a perfect match for certain senior positions within our strategy organization, and I told her so.

Wondering who to turn to for mentorship? Your best bet is to seek out, first, what's working exceptionally well within the company, and second, who's making it work. If you are not working within your target company or even industry, I suggest turning to a resource like LinkedIn to connect with experts who will be willing to advise you. Find individuals in your target industry or firm who have risen faster than average. What were their approaches to building their career? What can they share with you about their experiences? What pitfalls did they come across, and how did they avoid them? Truly understanding your industry and your company, and how advancement works within them, is critical if you want to maximize the returns on your career currency.

TICKET PUNCHES

Formulating the right career plan—as opposed to one that literally just looks good on paper—doesn't occur to many people until it's too late. They find themselves in senior positions but in a role or within a division of the company that doesn't lead to their end objective.

In the military, career moves that are "unofficially necessary" to reaching more senior levels are often called ticket punches. It's highly beneficial to complete certain assignments to become a general officer in the armed forces, and after you pass a certain point, you can't go back and experience those assignments. Over the course of my career, I've had the opportunity to speak with many members of the military, one of whom emphasized just how seriously those ticket punches are taken. They said, "If we see somebody who's getting all their tickets punched, we know leadership has plans for that person. It's clear when they're gathering all the experiences they need that they are likely to qualify for the most senior positions in the future."

The other side of learning your chosen industry's ticket punches (to use the military lingo) is finding out what *shouldn't* be punched. For example, in large companies, spending too much time on a single assignment at headquarters can make you less eligible for assignments in an operating unit. If you spend a long time in a highly technical field, you may not be regarded as qualified to take on a customer-facing leadership position in sales and marketing.

It's often the case that even when the dos of a career path are discussed, the don'ts aren't. You probably won't find a list of roles and projects to avoid posted on general career sites or printed in the company manual. This isn't the sort of knowledge you can glean from a list of rules. For this, and for much more, you need a mentor who will speak frankly with you about the *unspoken guidelines*.

TAXES AND TARIFFS: ANALYSIS PARALYSIS

It is possible for thorough professional planning to reach a point of diminishing returns and, even worse, obsessive indecision. While it is not only wise but necessary to seek out advisors, ask questions, and do your best to map your individualized route to success, it is equally necessary to continue moving forward.

If you find that "doing your homework" has become "panicking about making a mistake," it's time to take a deep breath. Remember that even the most successful people in the world didn't hit all the right milestones at the right moment in the right way—they learned as they went and occasionally made mistakes.

The best path forward always involves both thoughtful planning and occasional flexibility. Learn everything you can but remind yourself that you'll always have more to learn. Plan well but remember that you will still need to improvise when unforeseen opportunities arise. Analyze your career field carefully but don't let yourself become paralyzed. Paralysis will erode your career currency and hold you back from achieving your aspirations.

BALANCING PROCESS AND PEOPLE

When it comes to planning your advancement, it's important to balance a *process-focused* way of thinking with a *people-focused* one.

The *process* approach encompasses things like talent planning, leadership and technical development programs, corporate institutes, company-sponsored degree programs, and other training. The *people* approach, on the other hand, focuses on building relationships to help you progress within your organization.

Focusing too heavily on either approach can be dangerous. If you plan to advance solely on the basis of sponsorship and other relationships, you face the risk that the people you count on will be moved elsewhere within the company or will leave it altogether. If you concentrate only on following your organization's career development process, however, you won't enjoy the benefit of the right person putting in a good word for you at the right moment—and thus helping boost you into the right role.

I once worked in a division of our company that was led by a "larger than life" leader. He had personality, charisma, and a passion for talent. He also had a small cadre of high-potential employees he'd cultivated over the years. This team had ably tackled hard assignments around the globe.

This leader had little patience for structured development programs. He believed in assigning talented employees to difficult tasks that would grow their skills. Anyone could observe that his approach worked, and for his core cadre of talent, this was an effective career development approach. For the most part, these employees rose to director roles and positions of authority across various functions within the organization and were, no doubt, poised to assume vice president positions as they became available.

Then, the leader retired.

While these employees were all talented and capable, they had not focused much on our corporate processes or philosophy around talent management. They hadn't received a lot of exposure to other leaders within the company. They were regarded very highly within one segment of the business and were indisputably prepared to take on challenging problems. But they also had a reputation for being heroes and mavericks, just like their former leader. Under new leadership, the business took a more process-centric approach to succession for senior roles.

What this revealed was the value of full-spectrum leadership. For the roles of greatest responsibility, the company wanted people with a broad knowledge of the business, people as skilled in preventing problems as extinguishing fires, people who had participated in corporate leadership programs and obtained advanced degrees. Employees from this former leader's cadre had few of these boxes checked.

As VP roles opened up, these employees were passed over, with most of them eventually leaving the company for other interests. Their people-focused path to success had taken them to admirable heights within the company, but inasmuch as it excluded a focus on process, it also kept them from reaching the very top.

EXERCISE: WHAT'S YOUR OBJECTIVE, AND HOW CAN YOU GET THERE?

Once you've done your homework, your next step should be committing your knowledge to paper. Jot down what you've learned about the assignments and knowledge necessary to qualify you for the job you hope to have. Figure out what important relationships you need to build. These relationships could be with certain individuals who have knowledge and influence within the organization, or they may be with whomever occupies specific positions that will always operate as gatekeepers of the path you wish to pursue. Map out the pitfalls you could encounter along the way. Once you've completed this exercise, keep your notes handy. You will need them for chapter 3!

BE EXTRAORDINARY

Develop a Plan for Extraordinary Success

My sister Kristen has been an avid runner for years—it's part of her daily routine. And while she primarily focuses on her own goals, she rarely fails to offer a critique of the form exhibited by other runners.

This is a topic she has clear, firm ideas on thanks to the training she completed in preparation for her first marathon. The point her coach stressed to her above all others is that good form involves channeling all your energy forward, eliminating any side-to-side or other unnecessary motion.

Pursuit of an exceptional career is a lot like running a marathon. To maximize the value of your career currency, you need to minimize side-to-side motion. You need to ensure that each day moves you forward in your career—versus side to side or, worse, backward!

The best way to ensure that your movement is carrying you in the right direction is to develop a solid career plan.

If you've been through the preceding chapters, you should have a pretty good idea of what you want to do and how you want to apply that within a specific industry or company. Creating a career plan is where you put those pieces together.

HOW *NOT* TO PLAN YOUR CAREER

You have likely heard the quote that has been attributed to a range of famous figures from history: "If I had the time, I would have written you a shorter letter." Regardless of where this quote originated, it certainly rings true for letter writing, in the sense that less is usually more in order to communicate important information. The same holds true for career planning.

In my experience, the key to effective career planning is simplicity and taking the time to focus on the experiences and career moves that really matter. On more than one occasion, employees have approached me with extraordinarily complex charts—Venn diagrams, multicolumn spreadsheets, road maps that seem more like five-lane highways at rush hour—which they invariably credited as the path to a successful career. But, as I tell them, there's thorough planning and then there's structuring so rigid it can lead to missed opportunities.

TAXES AND TARIFFS: HAVING THE WRONG PLAN

Over the years I have seen many different approaches to developing career road maps and plans. Some are better than others, and the following example is one of the less effective approaches I have seen. It was provided to me many years ago by one of my mentees, so to respect the confidentiality of the original source, I needed to re-create it around a fictional identity.

I enlisted my daughter Samantha to help me with this task. Being an avid Harry Potter fan, she decided the best approach would be to create a career road map for an aspiring young wizard about to launch her career. We also researched successful wizards in leadership roles and learned that it can take eighty to a hundred years to reach these top positions. It is quite likely, then, that aspiring wizards may not be using the best techniques to maximize their career currency.

First, here are the positive elements of the plan:

1. The road map clearly defines where the young apprentice is starting today, as a graduating student.

2. It does a nice job of defining the requirements of future roles and thereby critical skills or experiences needed to be successful.

The drawbacks of a plan like this as I see them are these:

1. There is no long-term vision defined for the aspiring young wizard. The road map is looking toward six different career aspirations, many of which are substantially different or in outright opposition (Evil Wizard versus Wizard Rule Enforcement) with one another.

2. The plan does not address time horizon, so it would be difficult to measure success or progress against this plan.

3. The plan is very granular in nature and could lead to microlevel analysis of individual job moves (recall "Analysis Paralysis" from chapter 2) versus keeping an eye on the higher-level strategy.

4. The plan defines a mentor for each prospective career move, which is a good practice in general. Unfortunately, engaging with six different mentors in parallel while evaluating or pursuing disparate career paths is likely to yield a lot of conflicting advice that will further delay overall progression.

5. Visually, the plan takes a scattershot approach, branching out in all directions from the center, versus looking at more of a linear, time-based view.

An exercise like this may be useful to support the analysis I recommend in chapters 1 and 2, but it will serve to confuse and confound, more than help, to guide your overall career. When I was presented with the original plan from which my daughter created this example, I wasn't able to see anything more than a collection of disparate career options. I politely set the paper aside and asked my mentee the simple questions from chapter 1: "What are you good at, and what do you enjoy?" From there we discussed logical long-term objectives and next steps to get there. This helped clarify his focus and plans for near-term development as well as long-term goals and timelines. Today my former mentee is a successful executive and on a positive trajectory for future advancement.

Apprentice Wizard
Career Roadmap (Age 17)

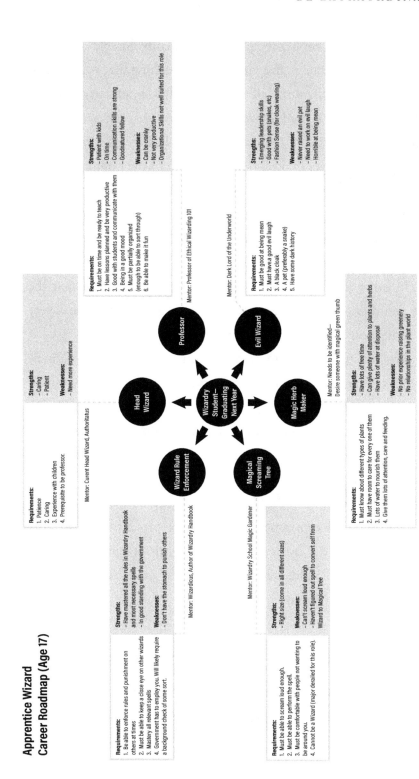

Requirements:
1. Patience
2. Caring
3. Experience with children
4. Prerequisite to be professor.

Strengths:
– Caring
– Patient

Weaknesses:
– Need more experience

Mentor: Curent Head Wizard, Authoritatis

Requirements:
1. Must be on time and be ready to teach
2. Have lessons planned and be very productive
3. Good with students and communicate with them
4. Being in a good mood
5. Must be partially organized (enough to be able to sort through)
6. Be able to make it fun

Strengths:
– Patient with kids
– On time
– Communication skills are strong
– Goodnatured fellow

Weaknesses:
– Can be cranky
– Not very productive
– Organizational Skills not well suited for this role

Mentor: Professor of Ethical Wizarding 101

Mentor: Dark Lord of the Underworld

Requirements:
1. Must be good at being mean
2. Must have a good evil laugh
3. A black cloak
4. A pet (preferably a snake)
5. Have some dark history

Strengths:
– Emerging leadership skills
– Good with pets (snakes, etc)
– Fashion Sense (for cloak wearing)

Weaknesses:
– Never raised an evil pet
– Need to work on evil laugh
– Horrible at being mean

Requirements:
1. Be able to enforce rules and punishment on others at times
2. Must be able to keep a close eye on other wizards
3. Mastery all relevant spells
4. Government has to employ you. Will likely require a background check of some sort.

Strengths:
– Have mastered all the rules in Wizardry Handbook and most necessary spells
– In good standing with the government

Weaknesses:
– Don't have the stomach to punish others

Mentor: Wizardicus, Author of Wizardry Handbook

Mentor: Wizardry School Magic Gardener

Requirements:
1. Must be able to scream loud enough.
2. Must be able to perform the spell.
3. Must be comfortable with people not wanting to be around you.
4. Cannot be a Wizard (major derailed for this role).

Strengths:
– Right size (come in all different sizes)

Weaknesses:
– Can't scream loud enough
– Haven't figured out spell to convert self from Wizard to Magical Tree

Mentor: Needs to be identified—
Desire someone with magical green thumb

Requirements:
1. Must know about different types of plants
2. Must have room to care for every one of them
3. Lots of water to nourish them
4. Give them lots of attention, care and feeding.

Strengths:
– Have lots of free time
– Can give plenty of attention to plants and herbs
– Have lots of water at disposal

Weaknesses:
– No prior experience raising greenery
– No relationships in the plant world

Nodes: Wizardry Student—Graduating Next Year; Professor; Evil Wizard; Head Wizard; Magic Herb Maker; Wizard Rule Enforcement; Magical Screaming Tree

How Not to Plan Your Career: This fictitious example is adapted from a real career plan that was shared with me years ago. To be successful, you must work from something more simplistic and focused on a single objective.

Plans should simplify the process—not convolute it.

You don't want to go into detail so excruciating that you grind to a halt. I addressed the pitfall of analysis paralysis briefly in chapter 2, and its importance is hard to overstate. When I'm speaking to groups about career planning, I illustrate this principle by standing in one small spot on a stage. I take a three-inch step to the right and then a three-inch step forward. "If you put yourself on this highly granular assignment-by-assignment career path," I explain, "you're not going to give yourself the maneuvering freedom to move in the general direction you want to go."

In other words, if you're too rigid, you may discover that the *path* you thought you were on is actually a *box*. And that, in a very real sense, you've boxed yourself in.

Another favorite quote of mine, attributed to Dwight Eisenhower, is "Plans are nothing. Planning is everything." This sums it up in my mind, because a rigid plan is only good until you begin the first step. There is no plan that can account for every outside influence that may come along, and adjustments must continuously be made. While establishing high-level waypoints en route to your goal is critical, so is flexibility.

The point of career planning is not a prescriptive plan that goes step by step, day by day, month by month. It's all about giving yourself directional guidance and allowing for a range of experiences that will lead you to your ultimate goal.

THE RIGHT WAY TO PLAN YOUR CAREER

When I was starting out on my own path, one of the early goals I set for myself was to gain experience with large-scale personnel management. A lot of organizations are matrixed in the sense that you might have project management responsibilities, but the employees—from a human resource perspective—are managed by another leader in engineering or another functional group.

So one of the things I wanted to make sure I did early in my career was manage a large group of employees as their actual personnel manager. Essentially, that entailed dealing with all of the issues that naturally arise within any group of people working together—the problems, the training, the disciplinary actions, the instances of poor performance, the promotions, the raises, the pay planning—all of these and many others.

Another goal I set for myself was managing business relationships with customers—an experience that would be critical to success in more senior positions down the road.

I set these first goals after taking a self-inventory, as outlined in chapter 1, and mapping my route to success based on my best understanding of the industry, as discussed in chapter 2.

As I did my homework, however, I learned that it was going to be important to demonstrate an ability not simply to manage existing business but also to secure new business for my company. By continuing to study the path to success in my chosen industry, I established an additional ticket punch that I viewed as necessary to realize my career aspirations.

This general goal of acquiring new contracts broke down into aiming for assignments in which I would have the responsibility to competitively pursue new work for the company. I knew that in doing so I would demonstrate not only a particular skill set but also an understanding of what the corporation was looking for in its next generation of leaders.

As a result of both my independent research and mentoring relationships, I knew what questions the company asked when it came to filling the most senior roles:

- Can these candidates secure new work to ensure a bright future for our business?

- Can they build strong relationships with customers?

- Do they consistently deliver results while also creating an energized and inclusive workforce?

I knew that if I wanted to realize my career aspirations, I had to set and achieve shorter-term goals that would lead to ever-greater opportunities. I hope that you can see, from my own example, how the information-gathering steps previously discussed will allow you to establish a useful career plan that maximizes the use of your finite career currency.

Now, let's break down the process of career planning into its most important components.

Look into the Future

You've now taken inventory of yourself and your preferred industry. In that process, if not long before, you probably acquired a vision of yourself in the future, at an advanced stage of your career. The vision may be blurry. It may exist at an indistinct mile marker in the years ahead. Now is the time to solidify this image—instead of asking yourself where in a general sense you want to end up down the line, give yourself a time parameter.

Remember to aim high—we are targeting extraordinary success! As I mentioned previously, this will look different to everyone. What is most important is that you define a professional vision that will stretch you and that may—in fact—seem almost unachievable from where you are today. Remember, this is a vision and objective for your future, and it can always be reconsidered down the line. The work you completed in your chapter 1 exercise will provide the foundation for this assessment.

Get Specific about Goals

Next, you'll need to define—as you observed in my story—the roles you might take along the way to become the person you foresee at the ten-, fifteen-, or twenty-year mark you set in the previous step. From experience, I know that the most effective approach to career planning starts with clarifying goals. Breaking the endless future into measured segments of time is a great way to do so.

Make sure you're not overly restrictive. Remember that establishing these goals is about providing yourself a variety of experiences that can work together to qualify you for your ultimate goal. Try to come up with three to five of these interim objectives to break your desired path into manageable segments. The notes you captured in the chapter 2 exercise will be the input to this process.

Identify Necessary Skills

Now you'll identify critical skills you will need to perform each target role you've set for yourself. If, like me, you determine that your highest ambition will require a demonstrated proficiency in acquiring new business, you need to look at what specific skills, habits, and characteristics would help you accomplish that. To excel at acquiring new business, you would need to know your business inside and out so you can confidently explain your capabilities and differentiators to prospective customers. You would need people skills. You would need the confidence to reach out to new contacts and not become discouraged at the first signs of resistance.

These are only some of the traits and abilities that would help someone succeed in pursuing new business. Carefully consider the nature of each goal you've set for yourself and try to come up with a similar list.

Consider Constraints

As valuable as it is to keep your abilities and aspirations in sight when setting goals, it's equally important to consider your personal constraints. What are you *not* willing to do?

Often, constraints aren't about personal preferences so much as priorities. There was, for instance, a time when I was finishing my master's degree in Philadelphia while working. I let the company know that for the years it took to complete my degree, I wasn't available for relocation. This was a short-term restriction I placed on myself for the long-term value of the master's degree. Completing an important degree, training program, or assignment may mean narrowing your options for now, but it's worth it if what you're accomplishing will pay dividends down the line.

TAXES AND TARIFFS: BE HONEST ABOUT CONSTRAINTS

From the very beginning of my career, I have tried to not have personal constraints—I've always wanted to remain open to whatever exciting opportunities come my way. At the same time, there have been sacrifices along the way. There have also been points in time where I needed to either pass on an opportunity or negotiate with my employer to make a job or work location viable for me.

While I always advise others to be as open and flexible as possible when considering next career steps, it's also important that you're honest with yourself and others about your constraints and personal circumstances. The point of career planning is to take you where you, individually, want to go. And while your professional goals are worth making sacrifices for along the way, they aren't worth compromising your values, your health, or other dimensions of your life outside work.

If certain work locations, degrees of travel, types of work, or work hours simply won't fit with you or your life circumstances, be honest with yourself—and be honest with others. It will serve you best in the long run.

Name Your Nonnegotiables

This is where you list out the ticket-punch items you worked out in chapter 2: What are the experiences you absolutely must acquire to be successful in the future? If you are working for a large corporation, this might be a crucial rotation through the headquarters organization or the corporate audit department. If you are a freelance artist, it may be a high-profile assignment with a top advertising firm. Whatever path you are on, there will almost certainly be a handful of these, and it will be wise to understand and plan to pursue them.

Plan for Failure

Did he really just say "plan for failure?"

Yes, I did. Let me tell you why.

If you truly wish to pursue an exceptional career, you will have to aim very high, as I mentioned earlier in this book. And when you aim high, that means stretching into much more responsible roles than you may sometimes be qualified for. This may be easier for some of us than for others.

Men and women, for example, are brought up in our culture to think about risk taking and failure in different ways. Reshma Saujani, the founder of Girls Who Code and best-selling author of the book *Brave, Not Perfect*, highlights the unfortunate reality of a culture that teaches boys to be brave and girls to be perfect. In her renowned TED Talk on this subject, Saujani points out that when translated into the professional world, the impact of this childhood programming is staggering. She cites the statistic that when applying for jobs, on average men will apply if they meet 60 percent of the advertised job requirements while women will generally only apply if they meet 100 percent.

Whatever your gender, it is imperative when setting your goals, and when navigating your career, that you aspire to the "brave" end of the spectrum. Aim high, take calculated risks, and learn from failures. If you approach your career in this manner, you will become accustomed to minor setbacks along the way, learn from them, and learn how to overcome them. You will, in large measure, avoid much more catastrophic failures that can diminish your career currency.

IT ALL COMES BACK TO CAREER CURRENCY

Terry has been my mentor for more than twenty years now—you'll read much more about him in chapter 6. He's passed along so many memorable nuggets of wisdom they could comprise their own book (and, for that matter, he's written two books himself). One of the earlier—and more memorable—lessons from him clarified for me the idea of career currency, and why it matters.

When I was twenty-eight years old, he sat me down and told me I was too old to ever run a large company. I looked at him like he was crazy. How could that be, when I was just beginning my career? Patiently, he walked me through his logic.

He began by starting at the top of our organization, with the CEO, and asked me what roles I might be expected to occupy before being qualified as a candidate to lead our company. He asked me for how long, and then what roles would qualify me for those jobs. As we talked through each of the steps in descending order and the time frame for each position, it became clear how far I had yet to go. And yes, on a standard timeline with standard expectations, I was indeed too old already to get to the top—even if I did everything right!

Of course, Terry was walking me through this scenario not to discourage me or to suggest I truly had no chance of reaching the top, but to impress upon me how far I had yet to go and the importance of working hard and staying focused on the right professional path to maximize my learning and accomplishments.

This solidified in my mind the value of my career currency and the imperative to spend it wisely. It also led me to be more flexible when leap-ahead opportunities presented themselves. In fact, the three biggest leap-ahead moves of my career were not contemplated in my career plan and were fairly significant deviations from what I had expected. But they offered opportunity to broaden myself, work for good people, and, most importantly, stretch into positions of significantly greater responsibility. Because I had thought more broadly about necessary experiences, I was able to recognize the benefit of these roles and say yes with little hesitation.

When it comes to career planning, the bottom line is this: it is important to keep in mind that the goal is not perfect execution of your road map; it is *extraordinary success*. Remember the words of Dwight Eisenhower—your plan should be used as a guide and as a measure of progress. And the most valuable thing to measure is your progress toward your ten-, fifteen-, or twenty-year goals against the timeline you've set forth.

EXERCISE: CHART YOUR COURSE

This is the capstone exercise for part I and the foundation of charting the course to extraordinary success. It is time to build your career road map. Remember my suggestions, and focus on high-level milestones with key experiences and candidate roles mapped out in between. You can use the format I have outlined below or come up with your own.

You can see from my example that I have kept it very simple. You may choose to add one or two additional rows to the format that cover items such as advanced degrees, professional certifications, or personal constraints. You may plan to start a family during a certain period of your career, for example, and want to pursue roles that involve less travel for a period of time. Just remember, this is intended to provide guideposts as opposed to being a rigid prescription. It is also something that should be revisited every year or so as your career evolves, always allowing flexibility for the unexpected.

As you complete this exercise, keep in mind also that your career currency is a subset of your life currency. Take the time to reflect on the objectives you've established and the skills you will need to develop. Understand the portion of life currency you will need to allocate to your career. Will you enjoy the journey? Will the rewards exceed the cost? This is the time for honest reflection and recognition of the investment you are about to make.

Career Roadmap: Engineering Services Executive

	Year 1	Year 5	Year 10	Year 15
	▲	▲	▲	▲
	Entry-Level Engineer	Leader of Others	Senior Leader	Top Executive
Key Experiences & Demonstrated Skills	· Product Understanding · Technical Proficiency · Basic Leadership · Basic Project Management	· Customer Engagement Skills · Engineering Talent Development · Complex Project Management · Cost Control & Financial Acumen	· Defining Vision and Strategy · Workforce Planning · Financial Plan Development · Client Executive Interaction · New Business Acquisition	
Candidate Roles	· Draftsperson · Lead Engineer · Team Leader · Associate Project Manager · Customer Liaison	· Engineering Department Manager · Project Manager · New Business Proposal Manager · Customer Account Manager	· Engineering Director · Division Director · New Business Director · Strategy Director	

Sample Career Road Map: You can download a blank Career Road Map template at www.jonrambeau.com.

PART II

TAKING ACTION

Now that you've taken the time up front to develop a plan for spending your career currency, it's time to move into action. By now you've been honest with yourself about your talents and capabilities. You've matched yourself with a career path that will yield professional success as well as personal satisfaction. Most importantly, you've thought through your approach to advance within that field.

In this section of the book, we'll explore a number of strategies to accelerate the early stages of a career, differentiating you from your peers and making you the logical choice for senior leaders who are prepared to place a bet on someone. These strategies don't involve a lot of waiting around. They are proactive and require going beyond the bounds of your day-to-day job description.

When I talk with early-career employees, the biggest mistake I notice is that they assume if they *do their job* very, very well, they will advance rapidly and find that extraordinary success they are seeking. While successful careers can be built solely through *doing your job well*, there are many, many others out there doing exactly that. To break away from the pack, more is required.

In this section, we will put planning into action, leveraging three proven strategies to build the experience, recognition, skills, and relationships necessary to realize extraordinary success.

Before you move from planning to action, here are some "rules of the road" that I recommend for anyone. These have guided me throughout my career and have at times been a lighthouse in a fog of uncertainty. While many of the topics in this section will serve to shape your professional brand, none will be as strong and enduring a reflection of your character as these three principles:

DIVIDENDS: START WITH THE THREE PRINCIPLES

1. **Integrity**—Above all, as you navigate your career it is very important to never engage in any behavior that could be construed as illegal or unethical, or that would compromise your personal values. Additionally, you must have impeccably high integrity in your interpersonal interactions. Honoring commitments, speaking the truth, and maintaining the trust of others will be paramount.

2. **Mission**—Notwithstanding rule number one, always place the interests of your business and its customers

before your own personal interests. While there may be times when this feels like an expenditure of career currency in the short term, in the long run it will pay dividends.

3. **Balance**—While this book focuses on your career, there are two other very important dimensions of life: family and self. It is important to always maintain a balance among these three dimensions as you navigate your career path, recognizing of course that there will be times when one requires more focus than another.

Keeping these guiding principles in mind, I like to think of your professional advancement strategy in terms of a pyramid, with your current job as the foundation. The three chapters of this section will build on that foundation, yielding a repeatable model that can be applied to each new role you assume along your career journey.

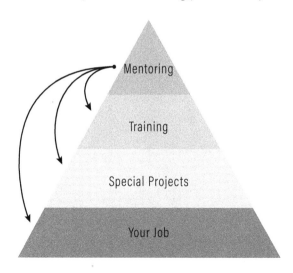

Your Professional Advancement Strategy: Each of the layers above Your Job represents a chapter of this book. Mentoring is your capstone activity and supports all other elements of the strategy.

CHAPTER 4

WRITE YOUR OWN SUCCESS STORY

Leverage Special Projects as an Accelerator

On the nation's longtime favorite variety show *Saturday Night Live*, there is a common problem involving new cast members.

When new actors come aboard as "featured players," their own fans wonder how the opportunity of appearing on *SNL* will expand their repertoire, while at the same time fans of the show itself wonder what new energy will come of this influx of fresh talent. However, months later it's common for both sets of fans to be wondering something entirely different: *Why* exactly were these new people hired? The downgrade from enthusiasm to skeptical curiosity stems from the fact that—all too often—new actors are relegated to barely there roles until they quietly leave the show and new talent is brought on.

This phenomenon can't be dismissed as lack of talent or a poor fit between the actor and the live format. One of arguably few things

Saturday Night Live has in common with major venture capital firms (see chapter 2) is the incredibly high level of talent and expertise required just to get through the door. The actors hired are clearly at the top of their game.

So, what's going on?

In recent years, multiple publications have provided a backstage peek into the process of *SNL* pitch meetings. This is the time when everyone from the cast and writing team gets together to work out what sketches will appear for the upcoming show. These meetings have been known to become so crowded that people are sitting on the floor and standing in doorways. It's easy to imagine how, in an environment like this, a new person might feel uncomfortable speaking up. However, it's when they do—when, specifically, they suggest sketches that showcase their talent while strengthening the show—that they're rewarded with more stage time.

As a new cast member carves out a presence by creating new material, the writing team gains a better and better idea of what they can do. While the cast member is wise to continue suggesting sketches, the writers themselves now have a clearer idea of how to best include them. Therefore, these actors are more likely to be featured in future shows. This may go a long way toward explaining why a relatively small group of actors tend to dominate the performances even when the full cast is loaded with talent.

While few companies operate on *SNL*'s pitch-meeting structure, there's a lesson here to be applied to nearly any career path: it's up to you to own your career and write your own success story.

THINKING BEYOND YOUR BOX

One of the challenges many employees experience early in their careers is a lack of opportunities to deliver results that reflect their full potential. What do I mean by this? When we hire new employees, we tend to focus on orienting them to the company and giving them simple, repetitive tasks meant to familiarize them with the business mechanics and culture. As a consequence, I find that most new employees wind up in a "helper" capacity—not responsible for anything in particular—or they wind up owning routine tasks that have neither beginning nor end, such as generating weekly reports.

While this is a safe and prudent thing for a first-line leader to do when assigning early-career employees, it can delay the company's ability to assess who can deliver and who can't—because these employees may not be truly tested for many years. This is done with the best of intent and allows employees to gradually earn more responsible positions. It can be frustrating, though, for those who wish to demonstrate their full potential.

I vividly recall two assignments from the beginning of my career:

Assignment One: As a new employee, I was tasked to receive updated quality assurance procedures for our manufacturing area. I was to review the changes and incorporate them into our procedure library—a cabinet full of binders containing paper copies of our most current procedures. When I asked for additional work to do, I was offered the opportunity to start converting these paper documents to a web-based format, and I did that in my spare time. To my knowledge, these documents were rarely accessed by anyone, because the members of the quality assurance team were all veteran employees who knew the procedures inside and out.

Assignment Two: This one was a little better. I was assigned to our production control team, where I was responsible for generating a weekly report of electronic components that needed to be shipped to our customers each week. I printed the report from our MRP system and then walked around the production floor to determine whether we could make the week's shipments. Next, I reported any disconnects to my boss. I would spend each week talking to production employees about making sure we met our weekly goals. As another boss was fond of saying later in my career, I was nothing more than a "shoulder tapper," roaming the area and reminding people to do their job.

If you step back from these two stories, you might well ask yourself how on earth either of these experiences would allow me to differentiate myself as an extraordinary employee who could be trusted to take on bigger and better challenges. If you're asking that question—you're right. These assignments weren't very helpful in that regard. Unfortunately, all too often that's where early-career employees may find themselves.

The good news is that there's an easy solution to this problem, which is to work with your company leadership to take matters into your own hands. If the job you're given doesn't present an opportunity to shine, you have to create that opportunity by going above and beyond.

CREATING YOUR OPPORTUNITY TO SHINE

The key to differentiating yourself in the workplace is to demonstrate that you are capable of delivering results and doing so in a way that has a meaningful and positive impact on the business. The best way to make this happen in your early career is to identify a business-critical need and lead a project aimed at addressing it. Taking on a challenge like this demonstrates initiative and understanding of the business. It allows you an opportunity to leave your mark, delivering a tangible outcome that you and others can point to as evidence of your capabilities.

It's important to note that taking on a special project like this must not interfere with your official job responsibilities. The most glaring error you could make would be to secure such an opportunity and then execute it at the expense of other responsibilities. If you're going to take this on, it's important to recognize that it's additive work and under no circumstances can your primary job performance degrade.

TAXES AND TARIFFS: BALANCING YOUR COMMITMENTS

Don't take on a project outside your primary job at the *expense* of your primary job—this would be an unwise use of your career currency and could set you back substantially.

When deciding what projects to commit to, it may be a good idea to return to the getting-to-know-yourself work from chapter 1—your abilities, limits, and specific skills you can leverage or strengthen. This will help you avoid devoting yourself to a project that may have a high profile but be too far removed from your capabilities or desired career path. The end result could be a drain on your career currency.

Many people within my industry have jobs working on existing customer contracts; we refer to these as programs. And while these programs represent their "day job," employees often have the opportunity to work on new business activities, such as creating proposals for new business.

At the same time, there's a certain belief bias I've run into among managers in the organization: sometimes they don't want their employees to work on proposal activities because they feel the employees' day jobs will suffer. These managers fear employees will ignore their day-to-day work, or start performing it poorly, due to the excitement—and sometimes the time demands—of pursuing new business. This is a legitimate concern, but it is a very manageable situation with the right understanding between leader and employee.

Therefore, I tell my teams this is absolutely the wrong attitude. We need to let people learn what it takes to secure new business because that's the future of the company. We need employees, and future leaders, who are capable of developing a new skill even as they continue performing diligently in their current work. It's true that attending to both matters effectively will require extra effort. The employees will need to put in some overtime hours and likely some nights and weekends for a month or two. But this doesn't mean they should be precluded from taking this on if they're willing.

If you run into a situation like this with your leader when proposing a special project, be prepared to provide a plan for managing your workload. Be specific about the steps you will take to ensure your primary job and the project work are delivered successfully. I've found that all good leaders are willing to be supportive when they understand the plan, the risks, and the enthusiasm behind a valuable initiative. More on the recommended substance of your plan is coming later in this chapter.

WHERE TO START

It can be challenging enough to effectively do your job when it's well established, but it is substantially harder to initiate a new project. However—as with previous steps—there's a methodical approach that will help you succeed.

I would suggest that you first absorb as much information as you can about the working world around you. What are the challenges faced by your peers? What keeps your boss up at night? Are there dimensions of how your office environment operates that senior management would like to see changed? Gather as much information as you can informally.

From there, a talk with your leader would be the next logical step. Explain your desire to help make a positive impact in the workplace and, at the same time, expand your skills. Express your desire to show them what you're capable of and offer up some initial suggestions on what projects you might like to take on.

Any enlightened leader should embrace such an overture from one of their employees and will in all likelihood respond favorably— perhaps even offering some suggestions of their own. The goal is to work *with* your leader to identify the right project that will help both of you make a difference. If your leader can help identify a project that would also be helpful to more senior leaders in the organization, all the better!

To give you a real-life example of how this can work, I'd like to share my first experience with this strategy.

In my second year with Lockheed Martin, I was working as a quality assurance supervisor. While I was now managing other employees, I was still performing relatively routine work and looking for the first opportunity to really make my mark in the business. I was part of a leadership development program, along with about a dozen other early-career operations employees. As a group, we decided we wanted to pursue opportunities to lead projects that could have a positive impact on our business.

We also engaged our program leader and asked for his assistance. He thought this was a great idea, going so far as to speak with several of the vice presidents within our division, spanning engineering, operations, finance, and human resources. All of these senior executives were supportive, returning to our leader a short list of project ideas—essentially, things within their domains that were troublesome to them and that nobody was focused on.

From this list of projects, we selected one from each executive, allowing our group to divide into four project teams. When making my selection, I deliberately chose to work on a project in support of our finance VP. This allowed me to build my acumen in the financial domain (which was a key skill within my career plan) and also to hopefully build a relationship with a respected executive to whom I'd had no previous exposure.

Once our team was formed, I volunteered to be the leader. I then spent the next six months or so working with my team members after hours to analyze overhead cost growth across our division. The highly successful project culminated in a brief to our senior executives on why overhead expenditures had been increasing, along with ten recommendations for reducing these costs.

Working on this project had several tangible benefits for me:

1. It offered an early opportunity for senior executive exposure, a critical ingredient in being considered for challenging new assignments. You can't be recruited for new challenges if leaders don't know you exist.

2. It offered a fabulous opportunity for cross-functional learning. I was able to expand my practical knowledge of the finance domain and build relationships there. This was essential in establishing myself as someone who was versatile enough to be dropped into another part of the business, get my bearings, and be successful with a challenging new task. This experience also built valuable skills that I would need in the future as I pursued my goal of becoming a general manager.

3. This was my first professional leadership opportunity. While I had begun to "manage" people in my supervisory role, this was my first real chance to take a team of talented professionals and lead them in an outcome-based endeavor—a critical skill to demonstrate if you are seeking early leadership opportunities.

4. This experience broadened my professional network. I built many new relationships with colleagues across the business—people I would never have met within my operations domain. In addition, I got to know some of our most senior leaders, and these relationships continued to pay dividends as I moved forward in my career. Whether I was looking for my next challenge or seeking a letter of rec-

ommendation for graduate school, these senior executive contacts were an asset that I was able to draw on regularly once the relationships were established.

5. Finally, and perhaps most importantly, this was an opportunity to leave something behind. The recommendations made by my team led to some changes in how our division managed its overhead costs, and we were able to leave behind some tools that allowed our finance executives to analyze these costs in a more thorough way. We left behind something tangible that we could point to in the future—evidence that we had truly had a positive impact on the business.

The main thing to remember when creating your opportunities is to make sure they align with your career goals and plan, once the work in part I has been completed.

IT'S ONLY GOOD IF YOU'RE SUCCESSFUL

It goes without saying, of course, that taking on a special project will only boost your career if you are successful and deliver a positive outcome. So, when you work through this process, be thoughtful about the ingredients you will need for success. While this list is not exhaustive, some basic recommendations are as follows:

1. Negotiate up front for the skills you will need. Assuming you will need others to assist you, it is critical to understand the work you'll need to accomplish and what skills will be necessary to be successful. As you negotiate the scope of the project, secure the commitment of your leader to make others available for the project.

2. Start early and plan for delays. A project rarely runs to completion without unanticipated challenges and delays. Be sure that when committing to timelines, you allow yourself some margin for error. If there's work that can be done early, do it—even if it puts you ahead of schedule— because you never know when you might hit a snag, or when your day job might flare up and pull you away from the project. Remember, you need to balance the project and your daily job responsibilities, so allow some contingency for both.

3. Set clear expectations with your leader on the desired outcome. I highly recommend you develop a project charter that includes the major work to be performed and the outcome that is desired. Agree on this up front with your leader or project sponsor. If possible, this document should include the resources required as well, so everyone is of one mind on the plan.

4. Finally, try to secure a sponsor, advocate, or subject matter expert to advise you as you go. Ideally, this person knows much about the domain in which you're executing the project and can act as an advisor or guide as you move forward. Someone like this can often help you avoid pitfalls, be they technical, procedural, or political.

CAREER BENEFITS

As I'm sure you've seen by now, taking on special projects early in your career can offer significant benefits. These early opportunities can lead to new and exciting challenges that accelerate your career journey and maximize the use of career currency.

To capitalize on the benefit of your project results, be sure to incorporate them into your résumé, and be prepared to discuss them during future career discussions and job interviews. It is also important to link these project experiences back to your overall career plan, identifying critical skills that have been gained through executing the project and how these accelerate your readiness to progress the plan.

When done properly, the inclusion of special projects into your overall career strategy will accelerate your learning, experience, and professional maturity, which will pay dividends as you seek to break away from the pack.

CHAPTER 5

GET SMARTER

Identify Training Opportunities that Will Benefit You Today and in the Future

Training is a critically important aspect of advancing your career and maximizing the use of your career currency. When I speak about training, I think about it in the broadest sense, ranging from degree programs to technical skills training and everything in between. There are three important reasons to pursue continuous learning as you advance your career:

1. Supplement your current role. It is always a good idea to pursue skills training that will enhance performance in your current job. This could be focused technical training that will allow you to perform your current role more effectively, or it could be training in softer skills that will benefit you now and in the future.

2. Demonstrate commitment. Pursuing training outside the bounds of your daily work demonstrates a degree of commitment to your leadership. They will see that you are not content with the status quo and that you are committed to broadening yourself.

3. Build credentials for future roles. In addition to supplementing your current job, many types of training are an investment in your future. For example, many companies prefer to see an advanced degree in business on someone's resume as one moves into more senior leadership positions. By planning ahead, you can build these credentials to ensure smooth sailing down the road.

If you've completed the career planning steps from chapter 3, you should have a pretty good idea of what skills and training may be needed as you move along your career journey. The trick is figuring out how best to acquire those skills and when is the right time to pursue them. As a general rule, I advocate the philosophy of "get it out of the way early," in the sense that you never want to miss a career opportunity due to lack of training or credentials.

There are many types of training available to everyone. Depending on the size of your company and the degree to which they focus on continuing education, this may include a broad spectrum of company-offered training opportunities. While it is by no means comprehensive, the following is a sampling of some of the most common opportunities that may be useful in accelerating your career.

ADVANCED DEGREES

This is an area where I spend quite a bit of time with most of the employees I mentor. Frequently, I get questions about when the best time is to pursue an advanced degree and whether it is better to pursue a technical degree or an MBA. The answer, of course, is "It depends." It depends on where you are in your professional journey and where you are headed.

If you are focused on a career in leadership, an MBA is most likely the best choice. If this is the path you are on, timing is very important. For me personally, I couldn't wait to get about the business of pursuing my business degree, and I started graduate school about two years after I entered the workforce. While I was able to successfully complete the degree and I learned quite a bit, I have often looked back and wondered whether I might have gotten more out of the degree had I waited a few years and brought more real-world experience to the table.

At the same time, I have to acknowledge the compounding effect of working full time and pursuing a business degree on the weekends. This was a significant commitment of time and would have been nearly impossible had I advanced further in my career and also reached the point where I had a spouse and children to think about.

If you are pursuing a technical career path, I would suggest returning for your advanced degree as soon as your life circumstances allow. Building your technical knowledge base early in your career will set you apart from many others while ensuring you have the right tools in the tool kit should the right job opportunity present itself.

TRAINING PROGRAMS

Much of the training that I've received over time has registered as so much background noise—in one ear and out the other. However, I've found that the more experiential programs, which offer opportunities to simulate what's being taught and which incorporate real-life case studies, tend to stick with me. Later in the chapter, we'll look in greater detail at the idea of different training formats benefiting different learners. For now, it's important only to consider the variety of benefits you can reap from professional training.

In some cases, the benefits are direct—fresh skills or pieces of information that can be applied to the job you have or plan to have soon. Other times the benefits are found in relationships you form with those in or outside of your own industry. Many training programs provide an opportunity to meet people from different geographies, different disciplines, different professional levels, and generally different backgrounds.

As I mentioned earlier, some training may be of even greater value several assignments down the road, and if you have planned as described in part I, you probably have a good idea where this may be the case.

There are many intangible benefits that come with unplugging and going elsewhere, interacting with others and thinking differently, and doing something unlike your everyday job. And that in and of itself has value, even if the content and the curriculum aren't always as helpful as you would like or as sticky as they should be.

Leadership Programs

Many major companies offer corporate leadership development programs. These can be long-term programs—one to three years in duration—and are generally reserved for the company's most promising talent at a specified level. I highly recommend pursuing such opportunities if they are offered by your firm.

When I was hired at Lockheed Martin, I participated in such a program. Spanning two years in total, it included four six-month rotational job assignments in two geographic regions with a curriculum of training courses that went on in parallel. Anyone who graduated from the program still had to be proactive about pursuing the right assignments, but they enjoyed a great deal of support and encouragement in doing so.

I jumped at the opportunity to participate in this program, because I understood that graduates were considered high-potential employees. This sort of learning prospect fit perfectly with my career plan—it was an investment of career currency I could feel good about.

Lockheed Martin offers training for other levels as well— for midcareer and even executive development—but this one was especially valuable for me because of its many benefits beyond just the leadership training elements. This program helped me rapidly mature my thinking about the company and precisely where within it I wanted to go. This was largely due to the rotational nature of the program that provided rapid exposure to a variety of work locations, responsibilities, and leadership teams.

When a program can offer you an enhanced skill set along with a greater understanding of your company and broader industry, it's an opportunity not to be missed. Unless your personal circumstances preclude it, I highly recommend accepting similar opportunities when offered. As a graduate of the program I described above, I now speak regularly to current participants, and I treat each of those speaking engagements as an opportunity to recruit talented employees who can become future leaders on my team.

Corporate Institutes

Many large companies also have corporate institutes that offer one- to two-week courses in everything from leadership to financial acumen to project or program management. These are typically offered based on merit-based nomination or a lottery system. Speak to your leader about what your company may offer, and find out how to get on the list.

Company Skill Certifications

Many companies also offer skill certifications in a particular career path. For example, in Lockheed Martin, we have programs for certification as a program manager or a new business capture manager. These certifications typically involve a mix of training and real-world experience that culminates in an application for certification. These applications are reviewed by a panel of accomplished professionals, and certifications are approved or denied based on the strength of the application.

Industry or Professional Certifications (PMP, PE, EIT, CPA, etc.)

Depending on your chosen career path, there may be one or more industry or professional certifications available to you. Different companies place different weights on these. In my company, internal certifications often carry more weight because they are structured around the competencies needed for success in our industry. However, I have colleagues in other companies where these industry certifications are "make or break" to practice in the profession. Obvious examples would include a professional certification for a certified public accountant (CPA), for those practicing in the accounting field, and professional engineer (PE) for individuals working in an architecture and engineering company.

OUT-OF-THE-BOX OPPORTUNITIES

In communities around the country, the FBI periodically offers an opportunity for community leaders known as the FBI Citizens

Academy. When I was based out of Orlando, Florida, one of the security professionals in the company—a former FBI agent—asked if I'd ever thought about participating.

I told him I hadn't. It wasn't immediately clear how it would relate to my primary work, but as my colleague talked about it, I became intrigued. So I filled out an application, complete with a large collection of security forms, and eventually was accepted to the program.

The Citizens Academy required me to attend night classes once a week for three months—three months during which I never found myself bored. One day we would be at a range, learning about firing weapons, and another day we would be studying pyrotechnics and explosives. We learned about cybercrime and crime scene forensics. I have to admit I never imagined in my lifetime I would be firing a real-life "Tommy" gun, just like a gangster from the 1920s. I was receiving the type of education you certainly don't get in business school!

It was fascinating to learn about law enforcement and its role within the broader community. And even more valuable was the opportunity to meet other community leaders in Orlando. I'd embarked on the training out of personal curiosity, but I discovered it had a professional benefit—I was now connected with like-minded community leaders.

My experience with the FBI Citizens Academy is an example of one of the most common benefits realized by those who remain open to outside-the-box opportunities. In this case, I forged connections with people deeply engaged with the community and from whom I knew I could learn a great deal. This is one of several reasons why it's beneficial to take a second look at training opportunities that—at first glance—seem irrelevant to your primary job.

Sometimes a training endeavor is worthwhile because of the people it will put you in contact with. Other times, the not-so-obvious benefit has more to do with long-term dividends. With a vast range of training programs out there, you're wise to pass up those that truly offer no advantage to you in your current or anticipated line of work. However, before you skip that next company-sponsored presentation, ask yourself if it's possible the information could benefit you down the line at a more advanced point in your career, or if the knowledge might bolster your current role by allowing you to take on additional responsibilities.

Eight years ago, I was offered an opportunity to participate in a corporate pilot program called the White Men's Caucus. When I received the email invitation, I'm sure I visibly reacted, wondering to myself, "Can you say that at work? Am I in some kind of trouble?"

"No, no, no," my boss assured me when I spoke to her. "This is a new program we're piloting. It's about embracing the diversity of our workforce and making white men an active part of that conversation."

I flew to the hills of Tennessee to a place called the Dancing Bear Lodge, where I met other white male leaders from across the company. The schedule was intense. For four days and four nights, we started at 8:00 a.m. and went until 10:00 p.m. We sat in a circle out in the woods and talked for hours. For me it was a huge awakening. We'd all grown up thinking of ourselves as individuals, and we were coming to the realization that we were part of a group called "white men," which came with what I came to understand as "privilege"—and that this is what other people saw when they looked at me.

The White Men's Caucus was an eye-opening experience. I came back energized and inspired to put my learning to good use. For a follow-up session called the Allies Lab, I participated with women and people of color. We followed a similar format of discussion with a more diverse group of perspectives and exchanged views on how to work more effectively with one another.

These programs were so successful that they are now conducted for all leaders in our business. Just this year, I was offered an opportunity to serve as executive sponsor for a shorter day-and-a-half version of the corporate training program. I leapt at the opportunity. As a sponsor, I opened up and talked about my own experience and how it has completely transformed who I am as a leader.

I've mentioned how important diversity in a company is—particularly from a leadership perspective. And while the caucus I've discussed here wasn't leadership training in a direct sense, it was training on a vital dimension of good leadership. If you're aiming for top leadership positions in your industry, keep an eye open for these opportunities that are less about the nuts and bolts of the job and more about broadening your perspective in a way that promises to make you a better leader.

Whether it is the FBI Citizens Academy, the White Men's Caucus, or something completely different, out-of-the-box experiences can be enriching, rewarding, and professionally beneficial. The value to be had in these opportunities isn't necessarily something you'd think of beforehand—it may not be obvious. But you're well advised to keep an open mind when evaluating a range of opportunities that could be helpful in longer-term and less apparent ways.

TAXES AND TARIFFS:
TARGET TRAINING THAT PAYS DIVIDENDS

While each training opportunity can yield meaningful professional growth, each requires an expenditure of your career currency. The modern world offers a truly impressive spectrum of learning opportunities, and you can easily go overboard. In addition to the array of in-person options, there are numerous online avenues to advanced degrees, certification programs, independent self-paced study, and individual courses—such as the MOOCs (massive open online courses) offered by many major universities, including Ivy League schools.

On one hand, it's great that virtual venues have eliminated many of the hurdles common to "brick and mortar" training institutions. In many cases, online learning can be worked into your schedule with a flexibility that traditional training doesn't offer. You don't have travel costs. It won't entail spending a week away from your home and family, staying in a hotel, or eating room service every night for dinner.

Given the apparent ease of it, online learning can appear to provide a simple solution if training opportunities have previously been prohibitive. Another characteristic they have, beyond convenience, is endless variety. As I advise with anything you undertake for career advancement, continue to be selective. You won't benefit yourself by signing up for every online certification seminar Google directs you toward, and you can end up overwhelmed and discouraged if you don't focus yourself.

Also, carefully consider the source. The same convenience factor that appeals to trainees applies to organizations that sponsor the training as well—not all online training is equal. Conduct some research on the credibility of any online training source you're considering. It's important to vet online sources to ensure both that the training you receive is rooted in valid experience and that your efforts will reflect well on you as your résumé is considered for future opportunities.

MAXIMIZING THE VALUE IN YOUR CAREER

To maximize the value of training, ensure it's linked to critical skills development from your career plan. It's also important to communicate the value of training you've completed to your leader—especially if it was company provided—to ensure that the value you've received is fully appreciated and to increase your odds of being selected for future opportunities.

Seek to apply your learnings to your job to fully unlock the potential of what you've learned and to translate the theoretical knowledge into practical experience. When leveraged properly, training experiences will magnify the value of your work experience and better position you to maximize the value of your career currency and realize exceptional success.

Another part of maximizing the value of training is making yourself aware of how you, individually, learn best.

For almost four years of my career, I ran a training and logistics business. Within my team was an organization dedicated to what we called "human performance engineering." Simply put, this is the science of learning. We looked at how people receive, process, and retain information. Through this work, I learned that certain mechanisms are generally sound ways to convey information and make it "sticky" to the learner. I also saw that certain mechanisms, despite the vast variety of people's individual preferences, just don't tend to work.

Generally speaking, it's the learning from hands-on experiences that people retain. Training programs that offer a combination of "classroom education"—whether or not it actually occurs in the classroom—and opportunities to put that new knowledge into practice are, for the most part, going to be the most beneficial.

That said, everyone has their own learning style and preferences. If you prefer to learn independently, keep up to date with the newest expert-authored leadership books or professional journals in your field. Others prefer an environment where there's a teacher to walk them through, for instance, the fundamentals of corporate finance. They want the opportunity to ask their questions on the spot and may thrive in a group-learning situation.

As you consider how you learn best, look at your preferences as *guidelines* for helping you prioritize rather than limits. Beyond any fees that may be associated with training events, you have to consider expenditures of your career currency. Your time and energy outside of office hours factor into career currency as well. You only have so much of it, and if you end up overspending (in either sense of the word), you might end up learning very little for your investment. This is a good reason to ask yourself not only whether the training content pertains to your career path, even in more subtle ways, but also whether the format, setting, and methodology would benefit you. Before you spend $3,000 on a course, learn what you can about it. Ask if you can audit for one session to get a feel for how knowledge is transferred.

Receiving training is important; retaining the information that you are provided in that training is even more important. Understand how you learn, and understand how you best absorb information. But regardless of how you best learn, don't forget that experiential training can be almost as much about making new connections as gaining knowledge.

CHAPTER 6

FIND A HERO

Unlock the Strategic Value of Mentoring and Sponsorship

Every day, my mentor Terry would walk into my office, sit down at the edge of my desk, and ask the same question. "What did you learn today?"

I feared that inevitable daily question at first. He was putting me on the spot, and I found myself scrambling to come up with one or more insightful observations. But as time went on, this predictable question began affecting the way I thought about things—not just for the duration of his visit but for the hours leading up to it. In contemplating lessons I could report to him, I was starting to notice just how many lessons an average day offered.

After a bit, I was nearly overflowing with learning points to offer up during those day's-end discussions. Terry continually challenged me to keep learning and growing. It's a habit that has stayed with me to this very day, and I have him to thank for it.

The last chapter of this section on taking action focuses on mentoring. As I mentioned in the introduction to part II, I view mentoring as a capstone activity, in the sense that it has the potential to enhance all other actions you take to develop your career and maximize the value of your career currency—be they related to your job, training, or special projects. The value of a mentoring relationship can vary considerably, however, depending on how you choose your mentor and how you manage the relationship.

HOW TO CHOOSE A MENTOR

When pursuing a mentoring relationship, it's important, foremost, to consider where this individual is placed organizationally. With perhaps a very few exceptions, it is recommended that you pursue a mentor within your company who has been an employee for at least a year. This individual would ideally be at a higher level within the same division you work in and approximately two levels above you (one level above your boss's level). If you decide to pursue someone outside your division, it is important that the mentor you are targeting have some knowledge of the division you work in.

The reason I recommend these criteria is that a mentor who meets them will be best placed to offer you meaningful advice. If you select properly, your mentor will be familiar enough with the part of the business you work in to provide informed counsel while still operating at a high enough level to grasp the bigger picture and offer a longer-term, strategic perspective on professional development and advancement.

Many employees I've worked with in the past have asked me whether they should be seeking their own mentor. Most large corporations have formal mentoring programs and use that process to pair high-potential employees with willing mentors. I've done it both ways, and in my experience, both paths to establishing a relationship can be fruitful. Overall, however, I've found the mentors I've identified on my own to have been more valuable because they were sparked by a sense of personal connection and mutual willingness to work together.

While mentoring can be a fairly clinical process and still be effective, I've always found the relationships to work better when there's a fundamental chemistry and personal interest on which to found the engagement.

One of the best mentoring relationships of my career was the first one I built. I was a new employee with my company, less than a year out of college. An early riser, I was accustomed to walking a darkened hallway at six thirty every morning to reach my cubicle in the manufacturing area. Every morning, upon entering the building, I noticed that one office was lit up. This was Tom, a second-line manager in manufacturing who also happened to be the site coordinator for our entry-level leadership development program.

It wasn't long before I would pause each morning and say hello to Tom, and not long after that before I would occasionally pop in to chat for a few minutes. Over time our conversations grew longer. Many times they were of a personal nature—we were both Corvette fanatics, for example—and other times they covered a range of professional topics. We talked about office politics, the longer-term path to advancement within the company, my career road map, and, most importantly, Tom's own personal experiences and career lessons.

There was no formal pairing process that led to my mentoring relationship with Tom. Instead, it grew naturally from common ground and mutual interest. The most valuable mentoring aspects of the relationship lasted about eighteen months, until I transitioned to another part of the company, but the connection with Tom is one I've maintained to this day, even as Tom has retired and begun his second career.

Whether you form a mentoring relationship as I did with Tom, through your own channels, or you are paired with a mentor through a formal program, your goal should be to liaise with a willing and engaged mentor. Preferably, you want to work with someone who is properly placed in the organization to offer you the critical advice and counsel you need for your professional development.

TAXES AND TARIFFS: MISMATCHED MENTORS

Don't settle for the wrong mentor. This isn't the most obvious pitfall on the path to success, but it happens more often than you may think.

It could be that your company pairs you up with someone and it turns out to be a poor match. Your assigned mentor could end up being at the wrong level or in the wrong part of the company, or they could simply be someone who doesn't have the necessary perspective to help you because they're not on course for high achievement themselves.

On the other hand, there may be someone who would be a great mentor for you at a later stage of your career—but not right now. I sometimes speak with entry-level employees

in our company who want to start a mentoring relationship. I always tell them, "I'm happy to have a career discussion with you, but if you want to meet with somebody on
a monthly basis, I'm not sure how much value I can offer
you." Their work is so far removed from me that I can't
offer much in the way of meaningful, practical day-to-day
advice.

When it comes to mentoring, don't aim too high too fast for
day-to-day practical advice. It's all about finding the right
person at the right time.

THE GIFT OF HONESTY

I had some apprehension about one mentor to whom I was assigned,
because he came across initially with a very stern demeanor. I
thought he would be intimidating and difficult to build a relationship with. I was wrong. Behind the gruff exterior was someone who
seemed to genuinely care about my professional development. What
came across initially as an intimidating personality was really just an
uncharacteristically direct style of engaging with people. In the end I
found that his frankness, openness, and honesty were incredible gifts
to a mentee.

He wasn't unnecessarily harsh, but he was forthright about the
good and the bad. Through his eyes, I was able to see how others
perceived me—how they thought about me, what they said when I
wasn't in the room, and what people really thought I would need to
do to improve as a team member and leader. My time with him ended
up proving so valuable that it helped me understand that honesty,
unflinching and unfiltered, was the thing I needed in a mentor above

all else. When you find someone who's as open as this mentor was with me, you can trust that they'll pass along real thoughts and observations instead of platitudes and benign encouragement.

What's more, someone who is frank by default tends to create a mentoring atmosphere in which you feel equally free to be direct. You need to know that it's safe to have important conversations—to share both your positive and negative views of yourself and the world in which you work. When this level of trust is established with a mentor, you lay the groundwork for a professional connection that can last for years and benefit you both.

Mentors are a great sounding board for career planning and professional advancement. They can also be great resources for working through more immediate problems. You don't want to walk into your boss's office and say, "You know, I really botched that report last week, and I feel terrible about it. Could you give me some advice?" That's exactly the sort of scenario you want to work through with your mentor. Especially because sometimes, read in full, the concern may be: "I feel like I failed on this assignment and I'm afraid talking to my boss about it will make the situation worse, but I could really use some perspective. What do you think?"

Depending on the scenario, your mentor might say, "I know your boss, and he did something similar five years ago. I've seen him be empathetic with people about this because he remembers what it was like, so I encourage you to talk to him." Or your mentor might say, "I know your boss, and he doesn't react well when team members make mistakes, so don't take it to heart if he reacts negatively. Here's what I recommend you do to minimize the fallout with him."

If this setup sounds familiar, you might recognize it from talking to an aunt, an uncle, or another neutral adult when you were growing up. Most of us didn't necessarily want to run to our parents when we'd made a mistake at home or at school—especially if it seemed probable that talking to them was going to make things worse.

It was quite likely another adult—acting in surrogate capacity—seemed just the right combination of friend and authority. You could be honest with them about your circumstances, knowing that they wouldn't judge you but rather extend sound, honest advice out of concern for your well-being. Ideally, you want to find a mentor who can deliver this same experience in a professional setting.

WHAT TO GET OUT OF IT?

A mentor can play many different roles as you seek to navigate the professional world and advance your career. These are the principal areas I've found to be important.

Political Guidance

As I mentioned earlier, a well-placed mentor is an ideal resource to advise on office politics and help form a strategy to stay out of trouble. While I've never advocated political maneuvering as a means to get ahead, a basic understanding of it is a necessary evil (more on this in chapter 9). If you don't have basic awareness of the political dynamic in your workplace, you can easily run afoul of someone's agenda. This is a topic I would recommend be discussed as part of any mentoring engagement.

Review of Your Career Plan

A mentor can help you consider your company's logical career progression paths and shape your career plan accordingly. Many of my mentors have suggested specific experiences or job assignments to round out my career development and better position me for future advancement. I've found that taking these suggestions has generally paid dividends.

Institutional Guidance

Recall my second point from the introduction to this part: mission. A mentor within your company will be immensely helpful in ensuring that your efforts are aligned with and in support of your company and your customers. It is wise to have a conversation on this topic with your mentor to ensure you are not pursuing your career in a way that works at cross-purposes with this important principle.

Experience Library

A well-chosen mentor will have learned many lessons in their career. You can draw on this experience and avoid repeating mistakes they've made. They will also likely have tips to improve your odds of advancement, based on their own personal experiences.

Act as a Sounding Board

Mentors can be a very useful resource when you have a difficult, and sometimes time critical, decision to make. Whether this is a choice between upcoming assignments, the resolution of a relationship challenge with a coworker, or stubborn challenges in executing your current role—a mentor can generally offer insight and advice. Just try not to overuse the relationship, keeping it in reserve for the moments when you really need help getting past a difficult decision or challenge.

Active Help and Support

Some mentors may be willing to actively advocate for you—a role often termed "sponsorship" in the corporate world. Not every mentor will want to do this, because it moves them from a relatively passive role as a mentor to a more active role in advocating for your future. But if your mentor expresses a willingness to do this, sponsorship is a very powerful way to build support for your professional advancement.

There are so many valuable benefits in a solid mentoring relationship, it's hard to roll them all up in a comprehensive list. But at the bottom line, a good mentor should challenge you to continuously improve while supporting your continued professional growth.

PROTOCOL: HOW TO MANAGE THE RELATIONSHIP?

Once you've identified a suitable mentor and established your immediate goals, following the right protocol will ensure you maximize the value of the relationship and keep it positive. The following guidelines will help ensure you keep this important relationship on track and paying dividends.

1. It's important that you always take the initiative. If you've chosen wisely, your mentor will be a very busy person whose time is always in demand. This person will be willing to make time for you under most circumstances, but you can't wait for them to contact you when you have a need.

2. You should always come prepared to a mentoring meeting. What does this mean? First off, never assume your mentor will recall the details of your prior discussions. They may be working with several mentees and will have a full-time job on top of that. To begin, you should come prepared to recap prior discussions you've had with your mentor. One of my most embarrassing mentoring moments was when I failed to do this and my mentor began walking me

through the next steps of a different mentee's career development. He was confusing me with someone else! I eventually had to stop him and redirect the conversation. We were both embarrassed, and it could have been avoided if I had opened with a recap of our last discussion. In addition to a recap, you should come prepared with specific goals and discussion topics for each conversation. Be as specific as possible to guarantee that you maximize the value of time spent together.

3. Discuss up front the frequency and location of meetings, and then take the initiative to schedule them accordingly. Never assume your mentor will take the initiative to schedule your next engagement. You should also discuss their level of comfort with calls and emails in between meetings. Is it okay to reach out in case of an unforeseen need for counsel? If so, how best to do that?

4. Honor the confidentiality of the relationship. This is critically important! A good mentor will share valuable insights into the organization and will likely share their own personal experiences and lessons learned. They will generally do this assuming you will protect their confidence. Do not betray this by sharing what they've told you with others—not even on a nonattribution basis! Your ability to protect the trust and confidentiality in the relationship is a sign of maturity and will be looked on favorably by your mentor.

5. Don't be discouraged by breaks in the relationship. Again, if you've chosen wisely, your mentor will be in demand and may occasionally become overloaded. I've had a couple of

mentors over the years who went "radio silent" for periods of time when their jobs became especially demanding. Your best bet is to seek some insight from others into their personal circumstance if they are unresponsive. After one or two failed attempts to engage and schedule meetings, it is best to offer some space until their workload lessens— then reengage. Continuing to press for their time when they have none left to give can wear on the relationship.

6. Finally, change mentors over time. As I've mentioned previously in this chapter, it's important to maintain a separation of about two levels between yourself and your mentor. As you move and progress within the organization, you will logically need to change mentors to maintain these ground rules. Ensure you keep your current mentor apprised of your plans in this regard. As you contemplate career moves, they may even be able to suggest good prospective mentors in your next role—even broker introductions. Your past mentors, over time, may become peers or even subordinates. Maintain these relationships in whatever form they take as you move forward. I myself have seen this cycle come full circle. One of my early-career mentors now works for me. Over the years, I've maintained that relationship and now have a trusted advisor supporting me who can offer insights and advice on key business decisions, from within the ranks.

I've mentioned my mentor Terry on several occasions now, and it's because of the vast impact he's had on my career and on my life. He's still a close friend, and every once in a while, I'll still call him up or we'll meet for dinner. Though he's been retired for a number of years now, I know I still have someone I can call when I need to say, "I'm having a hard time finding the right solution for this. Could you give me some advice?"

He's written a couple of books on leadership himself, and he still frequently refers me to the first one, titled *Principles of Effective Leadership*. Based on the problem I'm calling him about, he might say, "If you remember chapter 6 …" or "You need to go reread chapter 7." It's a testament to one of his many attributes as a sharp leader that he's committed the entire book to memory and can so easily guide me to the correct points of reference.

It's also a testament to how, when you have a mentoring relationship as long running and trust based as ours, you both tend to be on the same page—in our case, literally. Because I've known Terry so long, I can talk to him without much time spent on setup. He knows me. He knows my capabilities and professional experiences. Because of this we can jump right to a synopsis of the issue and discuss a plan of attack. With your most trusted mentors, this sort of relationship should be your long-term goal.

PART III

LESSONS I'VE LEARNED

Several years ago, I heard world-renowned author Malcolm Gladwell speak at a company event. To say he was entertaining would be an understatement. His remarks were riveting, especially when he spoke about "The 10,000 Hour Rule." If you aren't familiar with it, this is a rule he postulates in his book *Outliers: The Story of Success*. The underlying principle of *Outliers* is that extraordinary success isn't about who a person is but rather where they came from. It explores life experience and circumstance as a basis for success. And one of the most fascinating insights Gladwell offers is that truly exceptional people tend to reach their pinnacle at roughly ten thousand hours (ten years) of practice at three hours a day.

During Gladwell's talk, I immediately began drawing parallels to our professional careers. The ten-thousand-hour rule made perfect sense in the context of this book, in the sense that wise expenditures of career currency should maximize relevant learning and minimize the time required to rise through your field and find exceptional success. At the same time, it was apparent that there is no substitute for hard work and the years of effort to get there. In the third and final part of this book, I will offer some of my lessons learned along the way, in hopes that you can minimize unnecessary expenditures and secure your ten thousand hours of relevant experience as quickly as possible.

As you migrate from "Assessment, Planning, and Positioning" to "Taking Action," you will inevitably encounter challenges. One way to effectively squander your career currency is to encounter a bad boss, a thorny political issue, or a dysfunctional team—spinning your wheels for weeks, months, or more, trying to navigate the situation. Even more dangerous to the value of your currency is the risk that these situations could tarnish your reputation and hold you back from reaching your full potential.

While it's impossible to predict what exactly your circumstances will be or to offer solutions for every land mine you might encounter, there are a number of common challenges I've experienced over the years. By approaching each of them in a methodical way, one can minimize unnecessary expenditures of career currency while keeping your stress level to a minimum.

It is my sincere hope that these experiences will help you make the best use of your career currency by anticipating challenges and staying ahead of them or, at the very least, properly diagnosing issues when they arise and dealing with them quickly.

CHAPTER 7

AGE ISN'T EVERYTHING

Understanding the Age Factor

If you have started early and are spending your career currency wisely, you will eventually run into what I refer to simply as the "age factor." Your careful planning and acceleration of your career will take you to a point where you've acquired more responsibility and significance within your organization than is typical for someone your age.

If you are reading this book and are already at an advanced stage of your career, you may be fortunate enough never to have to worry about this chapter. If you feel that is the case, feel free to proceed to chapter 8. If you're not sure (or if you are but your curiosity has now gotten the best of you), please read on.

There are a few points I want to make clear as I begin this chapter. I've discovered these things to prove true time and time again in my observation of those who work with and for me:

- Age does not equal ability.

- Age does not equal aptitude.

- Age does not equal competence.

- Age DOES roughly equal experience (*relevant* experience is a different matter).

Unfortunately, the reality I've just outlined—particularly the first three points—may go largely ignored by the majority of people you interact with professionally. This is unavoidable, and the way you handle it will have far-reaching implications for your career currency.

Most major professional challenges you'll face will require you to carefully weigh pros and cons, evaluate the scope of the challenge, and assess the resources available to manage the situation. However, managing the age factor requires much more finesse than most. I've encountered many capable and intelligent people who were not able to navigate this chasm successfully.

I can't overstate the importance of this: if you're going to accelerate toward senior positions relatively early in your career, you *will* deal with others' perception of your inexperience. Correctly responding to this pressure is a fine needle to thread. If you embrace and own that inexperience too much, you'll be dismissed as not ready. If you ignore the perception, push forward with bravado, and pretend to be an expert at everything you do, you'll be discredited.

It's a tightrope—you're balancing between a big danger zone to the left and another to the right. To the left, you're judged as not ready. To the right, you're seen as overconfident and underqualified. And right down the middle is the narrow path we're going to discuss in this chapter—the path of maturity.

In this chapter, you'll learn how to combine and leverage the experience of others so you can build an effective, high-performing team. In doing so, you'll not only learn to bring together people with the right experiences to create a team that's better than the sum of its parts, but you'll also ensure your own career planning efforts are not wasted. You'll learn to make a positive and balanced impression that will cultivate trust in your leadership abilities and business judgment, leading to greater opportunities ahead.

I place my recommendations into two categories, the first of these being the steps you can proactively take to minimize the negativity sometimes brought on by youth, while finding in it some advantage. The second category involves reactive steps you can take to manage the situation when your expertise or qualification is questioned because of your age.

BE PROACTIVE

The first topic I will cover is positioning yourself to be viewed as highly competent at any level, regardless of your age. While doing these things won't completely eliminate the age factor for you, they certainly will go a long way toward minimizing the effects and toward ensuring that the age factor becomes nothing more than a transient concern for someone who hasn't worked with you before. By following this playbook, you significantly increase the odds that your colleagues will see past your age to the capable professional you are.

Surround Yourself with Relevant Experience

There simply is no substitute for relevant experience when it comes to reliable and consistent professional decision-making. If you advance rapidly in your career, chances are you will have less overall experience (total working years) than many of your colleagues. To compound the problem, you may have moved from one organization to another while advancing, rendering some of your experience less relevant to your current organization.

To offset issues such as these, you must ensure you build a network of relevant expertise to draw upon in every role you occupy. In this way you'll ensure that adequate experience factors into your professional decision-making. This requires you to look at yourself with a certain degree of humility and realism and, most importantly, to acknowledge that you don't know everything.

While I was still a relatively new vice president in my company, I'd been working in our corporate headquarters in Bethesda, Maryland, when I was recruited to join our aircraft business in Fort Worth, Texas. This branch of the company had a notoriously closed culture. If you hadn't grown up in the business, it was hard to earn respect there. Many senior executives who transferred in were unsuccessful.

Going in, I knew I faced an uphill battle. I had been asked to lead the international portion of our largest project, a multination fighter jet development project that had encountered some challenges. I entered the role as a senior executive with no aviation experience and very little international business experience. How would I ever succeed in that environment?

On my first day of work, I assembled the leaders who worked for me. While everyone was courteous, you could almost hear the thoughts bubbling behind their skeptical demeanor—"Who is this young guy they've sent from corporate to lead us down here?" I knew that how I handled the first interaction would make or break my ability to effectively guide the team.

When it came time to address the group, I first told them a little about my background. The major experiences of my career so far. My style as a leader. Some of the professional challenges I'd faced in the past. Then I paused and got frank with my team. While I don't recall what I said verbatim, it was close to the following:

"I know you're all probably wondering why I'm here. I haven't grown up in this business. I don't have an aviation background. And I don't have much international experience either. You all are the experts in what you do—not me. If we are to be successful as a team, I am going to need to rely heavily on your extensive background and experiences in these areas.

While I know I don't have the experience you have, I do bring a fresh perspective to this role, and in the past, I've found I do have the ability to bring together a group of experts to make sound decisions and realize success. You have my commitment that as your leader I will bring every bit of my experience and ability to the table every day to help us make the best possible decisions as a team.

I will advocate for the resources and support we need to be successful. What I ask in return is that you lend me your advice and counsel—let me draw upon your expertise. If we can agree on that, I am confident we will be successful as a team."

This approach worked. And it may have been the only one, under the circumstances, that would have. I acknowledged the elephant in the room. I was honest with the team about my lack of relevant experience, but I also highlighted what abilities and experience I brought. I committed to act in the best interest of the team and, in turn, asked the same of them. Getting off on the right foot set the foundation for several successful years in our aircraft business.

Consider Your Image

There's an episode of the long-running sitcom *Frasier* titled "The Great Crane Robbery," in which the radio station where Dr. Frasier Crane works is bought by a young Silicon Valley tycoon—someone who's acquired career success, influence, and high-level responsibilities at a young age via the launch of a popular search engine.

As the two discuss Frasier's radio program at his apartment, the title character offers his youthful new boss, Todd, a glass of fine sherry to drink. The exchange that follows speaks to a less frequently discussed challenge faced by a young person who has rapidly advanced.

> *Todd (in response to the offered glass of sherry): Nah. It'd be wasted on me. I don't know the first thing about that stuff.*
>
> *Frasier: Oh well, in the great scheme of things, it's not really very important.*
>
> *Todd: It kind of is. I mean, ever since my search engine went public, people have been inviting me to fund-raisers and banquets. They expect me to know all sorts of things about art and music, wine—I don't know jack; it's embarrassing.*

In your own career, you may not find yourself at banquets where you have to talk your way out of discussions about Beethoven or Bordeaux, but this scene demonstrates an underlying reality of the professional versus personal lives of young leaders. If you're advancing quickly, chances are your personal life is not on par with your peer group at the office. At many points along the way, I have found that my life outside work has not kept pace with my professional progression.

While I don't advocate modifying your personal life to the point that it's no longer satisfying to you, there are some simple things you can do to minimize negative perceptions about your age and maturity.

One easy way to positively influence others' perception of you is to be mindful of your appearance. Factors such as dress, hairstyle, and jewelry all play into the perception of your professional maturity. Spending the money now to upgrade your wardrobe and other aspects of your physical appearance will likely prove a wise investment. You want to aim for a look that's appropriate to the peer group you currently reside in and any you wish to join in the future.

For the most part, the peer groups associated with various levels of company leadership adopt an unofficial dress code that encompasses broad characteristics such as *tidy, coordinated,* and *well groomed.* You can still embrace style choices that express your character—you're just well advised to make sure they fall under the umbrella of *professional appearance.* When your clothing has a timeless rather than an ultratrendy bent, when your pants and suit jacket are pressed rather than rumpled, when your accessories are tasteful rather than imposing, you give the impression of someone who, to put it simply, "has their act together."

DIVIDENDS: DRESSING (COMFORTABLY) FOR THE JOB YOU WANT

I should note at this point that I am a huge inclusion advocate, and there is nothing more important than having the flexibility to bring your full self to work every day. You should always look for this in an employer. At the same time, like it or not, people are all individuals. Bosses, peers, customers, and other business associates will all make judgments (conscious or otherwise) about you based on appearance. This should always be factored into your thinking before you walk out the door in the morning.

Fortunately, more workplaces are now prioritizing inclusivity and recognizing that a variety of appearances can fall under the umbrella of "professionalism." You want to look clean and put together for work, but that doesn't mean having the stamp of corporate America on you.

No matter what you do to dress for the job you want, make sure you can always look at yourself confidently in the mirror and be proud of what you see looking back at you.

The popular counsel to "dress for the job you want" has gained such traction for a reason. I would expand that notion to account for your current job as well. The big thing—the truly important thing—is not to dress for a job you've already advanced beyond.

Another aspect of being mindful of your appearance is engaging in activities outside the office that are "age appropriate" for the professional peer group you're part of or wish to be part of. If you're early in your career, this may mean swapping out a weekend pub crawl for a wine tasting. It may mean taking up golf—although I've never been able to take this one seriously myself. If you take up hobbies and interests common to the peer group you aspire to join, it makes you that much more marketable to the people who will make these decisions.

In this realm, as in so many throughout my career, I benefited from a mentor who was direct with me. This one told me I looked even younger than I was—and it would affect how seriously I was considered for advancement. He told me that in a different era, he would've recommended I take up smoking a pipe. Fortunately, the age of pipe smoking being associated with workplace maturity has passed, but I appreciated the spirit of the advice. From there, I took steps to look and act the part of the executive I was striving to be.

Focus on Courteous Confidence

As a young professional who's experienced early-career success and rapid advancement, it's easy to feel you are on track for a senior executive role and, as such, to feel you should be offered preferential treatment and advancement opportunities.

I can assure you that an attitude of entitlement is one of the worst you could adopt. It will not bode well for the future of your career. It's important to be gracious when you are offered a new challenge or favorable prospect and to respect and seek counsel from your coworkers who have more relevant experience than you. My advice is to execute each new role you are offered with diligence and to strike the right balance of humility and confidence in your own abilities. When I speak to new leaders, I always introduce the term "courteous confidence" as the behavior they should strive for. It's important to demonstrate confidence in one's own abilities and aptitude but equally important to do this in a gracious and respectful style that exudes maturity.

Always Use Sound Judgment

At the bottom line, one of the most important evaluation criteria I apply to members of my team is their judgment. Most importantly I consider their business judgment, but this is a skill that must be applied both inside and outside the workplace. And in this day and age, both of those can affect your career.

Consider the aspiring professional who posts less-than-flattering or even downright inappropriate pictures of their weekend antics online for coworkers to discover. Or the more traditional case of a rash business decision made on limited experience that causes the company financial or reputational harm. Yes, demonstrating sound judgment across the board is critical to mitigating the age factor and to advancing your career.

If you have risen quickly and are looking to demonstrate sound judgment in decision-making, this is a tremendous opportunity to reach back to the first point of this section and *surround yourself with good people*. As I pointed out at the beginning of this chapter, the more years of experience a person has, the more they have seen go both right and wrong. It is important that you find the right experienced team members to draw upon to evaluate important decisions from a variety of perspectives, carefully consider alternative points of view, and make an informed and well-supported decision or recommendation.

To underscore this point, consider the situation of a wildly successful tech startup company led by a charismatic young CEO. We need look no further than a company like Facebook, for example. While these visionary leaders earn the lion's share of public attention, there is typically a less visible but no less important companion to the CEO. Often when these companies "make it big," it is common for a very seasoned and experienced senior executive to join the management team of the company. Their primary role isn't to help establish the vision for the future—the CEO and founder will have that well in hand. Their role is generally to bring their wealth of experience running the mechanics of a large corporation—something a widely successful twentysomething visionary just hasn't acquired at the early stages of their incredibly successful career.

TAXES AND TARIFFS: LISTEN AND LEARN

You can do everything else right. You can move rapidly up your career ladder. You can prove yourself talented, capable, smart, and personable. But if you don't take the time to stop, respect, and draw upon the expertise of the people you work with, you'll overspend in career currency and sometimes exercise judgment that is less than sound.

When I took my first management position, I was asked to lead a team of people who were somewhere between two and three times my age, all of them hourly workers in the factory. Usually, on principle, they'd immediately reject someone like me—someone fresh out of college who, in many cases, could be their grandchild. Yet I was able to earn the respect of that team.

I accomplished this by day in and day out sitting down with them, getting to know them as people, and—most importantly—understanding their professional experiences. Even though they had done the same factory job for twenty, sometimes thirty, years or more, they had seen and learned a great deal. The fact that I listened earned me their respect and, in turn, their trust.

Inasmuch as they were paid hourly and were members of different labor unions, there wasn't an obvious incentive for them to want to do a better job, except for pride in the team and respect for their boss. I understood this because I invested time in understanding them, and from that point, I was able to motivate them.

Often young leaders come in with big goals and even bigger ideas. They perceive a need for change, and they're gung ho to see it through. But even if a sweeping, optimistic change is warranted, leaders benefit immensely from the knowledge and wisdom of those who have covered similar ground many, many times in the past. By taking the time to listen to those who have the experience you personally lack, you'll keep day-to-day operations running smoother, and you'll maximize the effectiveness of whatever changes you implement.

KNOW HOW TO REACT

While the proactive steps above will help ensure you are taken seriously, rapid professional advancement will undoubtedly lead to situations where you are discounted by others based on your age. Reacting in the right way is critical if you are to earn the respect of the more experienced professionals within the ranks. As opposed to the list of dos under proactive steps, here you'll read about two critical don'ts for reacting in a way that solves problems and does not create new ones.

Respond with Grace

The worst thing you can do when you find yourself being discounted because of your age is to become indignant. Handling the situation with a mature and professional tone is always the best course of action. In most circumstances, this means not directly addressing the perceived slight. In most cases, if you ignore the behavior and continue performing as a competent professional, you will earn the respect of those around you and over time realize career gains that are consistent with your ability and aptitude.

Dozens of times, I've gone to a business meeting with other members of my staff just to have my counterpart from another organization search the faces of my subordinates, trying to identify the boss. So often they've been sure it couldn't be me—not when I was clearly the youngest of the group.

I would be lying if I said this behavior never frustrated me. On the contrary, I think it's given me a little insight into the way many women and people of color must feel when they're similarly deemed unlikely to be the boss because of gender or race. If—or rather, when—it happens to you because of your age, it's important not to broadcast your irritation. The worst thing you could do is behave like a petulant child who feels disrespected. Instead, introduce yourself, state your role, and proceed with your business.

When you can handle someone else's professional faux pas this way, you exhibit maturity as well as confidence that your abilities speak for themselves. Depending on how obvious their mistake, the person who's disregarded you may feel embarrassed; they may feel they've insulted you and understand that they were in the wrong. They certainly *won't* have this realization—or potentially reflect on their own automatic age-based judgment of others—if you react with a tantrum.

Don't "Wing It"

You are sure to encounter circumstances where you simply don't have the relevant experience needed to offer an informed opinion or make a sound decision. In these times, you have to resist the urge to offer your perspective or make a decision without being fully informed.

From personally being there many times over the years, I've found the best response is honesty. If the best person to take charge on a certain decision is someone with more practical experience in the domain in question, acknowledge that. If you aren't informed enough to make a sound decision, be open about it. If you're part of a discussion and you're not familiar enough with the topic to contribute, either ask questions or simply listen and learn.

One of my favorite sayings—one I've embraced heavily over the years—is, "You can remain silent and let them think you're stupid or open your mouth and remove all doubt." There's nothing wrong with just listening to what others have to say. Indeed, listening is one of the traits of a truly effective leader.

Mandy Gilbert, founder and chief executive of Creative Niche, points out that admitting you don't know something can help you become a stronger leader because it promotes collaboration, empowers employees, and makes you relatable. For *Inc.* magazine, Gilbert writes, "From social media trends to coding languages, it's impossible to understand jargon from every department. So the next time you're being presented reports, interrupt and ask your team to explain any terms you don't grasp instead of hoping that the lack of understanding won't become an issue in the future. It always will."

Fortunately, it seems that the broader workplace environment is starting to value those who admit when they don't know something. Business experts with *Forbes* and *Harvard Business Review* have written about it, and the authors of the wildly popular book *Freakonomics* have covered it on their podcast. None of this increased attention means it's suddenly easy to admit you don't know something, but it does indicate an atmosphere of greater appreciation for those who don't try to pretend they always have the answer. In most cases, confessing that you don't know doesn't mean sticking your neck out, risking the respect of your associates, or destabilizing your career. In most cases, the benefits will clearly outweigh any perceived negatives.

A less obvious benefit of publicly saying that you don't know about a certain topic is that you establish yourself as someone who uses sound judgment. When someone seemingly has a quick, ready answer to any predicament, they promulgate the idea that any issue has a simple answer or, at the very least, that solving quickly is more important than solving correctly. Whether they mean to or not, leaders who "always know" encourage their staff to solve with speed rather than accuracy, even if it means ignoring nuance, and thus to be less effective problem solvers than they ultimately could be.

It is hard to understate the gravitas of a thoughtful, analytical leader who takes appropriate (but not excessive) time to gather additional information, listen to competing perspectives, and formulate a well-founded plan of action. The time dimension here would obviously vary based on the significance of the decision, but in no case can you allow a rushed decision to compromise the integrity of your professional judgment.

The main benefit of using sound judgment, as it pertains to our discussion here, is that you'll show your coworkers and subordinates that you value their experience and consider their input a critical component of the team. However, its other benefits include helping you demonstrate that you are a mature leader who respects the complexity of various workplace questions, is comfortable with your own knowledge and experience, and puts well-considered solutions ahead of having all the answers.

CHAPTER 8

KEEP IT PROFESSIONAL

Remember That It's Just Business

Negative emotion can kill your motivation. It can also kill your career.

Yes, negative feelings are life, or at least a significant slice of it. You may get passed over for a promotion or an exciting new assignment. You may be unfairly (or fairly) criticized for the quality of your work or your degree of perceived commitment. You may not receive the recognition or respect you feel you deserve. These experiences are hard to take in stride, especially when career advancement is a high priority for you. We can always justify negative emotion. But when you force those in the workplace to deal with yours, the potential opportunity cost—the deduction from your career currency—can be substantial.

It's natural to feel disappointed, frustrated, and even outright angry when you encounter professional setbacks. There's nothing wrong with feeling these things. The problem comes into play when you allow these emotions to linger and to take the reins. Even worse is when these feelings become evident to your colleagues. You must take disappointing moments in stride—learning from each of them and remaining focused on what I think of as the "Long Game."

While controlling emotions is a useful lesson for any professional, it's especially important for someone early in their career and seeking to accelerate it. Displays of emotion—especially the negative kind—are often construed as evidence of professional immaturity. And such displays are too often and too freely made by early-career professionals when things don't go their way. When you vent to colleagues about a professional disappointment, you can count on its being circulated among others in your workplace and eventually reaching your bosses. When it comes time for the next assignment or the next promotional opportunity, this is the sort of thing that will be taken into consideration.

In addition to signaling immaturity, outbursts of negative emotion can be taken as a sign of someone who's neither very composed nor reliable under pressure. Looking back over my career, I can recall numerous examples of individuals who did not handle disappointment well—and who saw their careers suffer as a result.

One extreme case involved the leader of a project team I served on. He was famous for lashing out when things weren't going his way and, specifically, participating in conference calls where he would erupt at the slightest hiccup. Having a front-row seat to his behavior for over a year, I wondered if—or rather, *when*—it would catch up with him.

I remember the moment when it did quite vividly. The team was giving a weekly status update, via conference call, on the progress of the project, and it turned out one of the employees had had a fairly unproductive meeting with a client. With the best of intentions, this employee tried to explain the situation for our notoriously hot-tempered leader. The employee was forthright about the client meeting not having gone according to our expectations and the client not accepting our proposal. He was in the midst of discussing how we would need to come up with a different plan when the team leader exploded.

As his face grew red and his voice climbed to a crescendo, he spoke in a derogatory way about the client in front of the entire team assembled, virtually, by phone. He didn't realize that his boss had walked into the office of one of the employees on the other end and was standing there listening to his tirade. He was not only disparaging the client but using some highly inappropriate language while he did.

He was removed from his position within weeks. Shortly thereafter, he left the company altogether.

While this is an extreme example, it can take much less to brand you as someone who isn't up for the task due to a lack of emotional maturity or stability.

If you're a naturally analytical, calm, and thoughtful person—great. You're probably going to do just fine. However, I imagine there are plenty of readers for whom this isn't the case, which is okay. It simply means that you'll need to develop a mechanism to keep your natural reactions in check. The options for accomplishing this are seemingly endless.

DIVIDENDS: PERFORMING A MENTAL SCAN

You could do something as simple as taking a deep breath or go for a slightly more sophisticated response such as the "mental scan." Andy Puddicombe, the cofounder of meditation app Headspace, suggests that when negative emotions have been triggered, we should conduct a brief mental body scan, top to bottom. "By shifting the focus to physical senses, you are stepping out of the thinking mind and bringing the mind into the body, which immediately has a calming effect," Puddicombe says. Speaking of Headspace, if you're someone who appreciates meditation, technology, and especially the intersection of the two, there are now many applications, many of them free, that offer quick guided meditation sessions along with other mind-calming aids.

You may just need to count to ten. You may need to walk away from a situation, take some time, and come back mentally refreshed. You may need to find something that can make you laugh—a good, healthy laugh is a great way to "switch tracks."

It doesn't really matter how you calm down and get control of your emotions—it matters that you do it. I've seen too many individuals who are otherwise very talented derail their careers because they weren't able to control their emotions. In turn, judgments were levied against them. Justly or otherwise, they were deemed impulsive, unpredictable, or disruptive.

Company leaders want people in executive positions who, among many other qualifications, are careful and thoughtful about their decisions. When it comes time to fill a senior role, they don't want someone who's emotional, because their emotional nature becomes cross-referenced with impulsiveness. The employee who whines over minor mistakes and yells over bigger ones is seen as someone who will make snap decisions, who will demoralize their team, and who doesn't have the patience to think through important decisions.

What I've covered so far in this chapter addresses what *not to do* when things go awry. Now you might be wondering about what you *should* do when faced with professional disappointments. In my experience, there are two courses of action that are successful, and which one you should use depends on the situation.

1. ADDRESS IT WITH PROFESSIONALISM

When met with a disappointment that requires you to respond, it's important to do so without emotion. Consider the facts and circumstances, and think through your response before engaging.

A simple example from my career involves a time when I was tasked by my boss to take responsibility for some additional duties that had previously been performed by one of my peers. While I was prepared to take on these new duties, my colleague didn't seem to want to give them up. It would have been easy to get angry with this person or to go running to my boss and cry foul. Instead, I created a plan to force a professional discussion with the boss.

I created a visual breakdown of work between myself and my peer. I included the areas of overlap between our roles and mapped out detailed work tasks that would fall to either me or my peer. I explained to him that we needed to resolve the disagreement and that I was going to schedule some time with our boss to review progress on transitioning the work assignments.

While this resulted in some debate about specific tasks, it had the desired result. Once we both knew a review with our boss was on the horizon, I was able to draw my colleague into a collaborative dialogue on how to accomplish the new division of work between our teams. By the time we met with the boss, we shared a common view of work distribution, and everyone, especially our boss, was pleased that there was no longer a disagreement to resolve.

2. FALL BACK AND REGROUP

There are other times when it may not be advisable, or even possible, to tackle the situation head-on. Sometimes you may find it necessary to quietly accept the disappointment, learn from it, and evaluate options to revisit the situation in the future. In other words, to play the Long Game.

Perhaps the clearest example of this occurs when you find yourself stuck working for the wrong boss (we'll discuss bad bosses in greater detail in chapter 11). In my career I have been blessed, for the most part, to work for exceptional leaders, but I've still had a few who were not. You could wind up in a subordinate role to someone who feels threatened by a young, capable employee or simply does not see the value you are able to offer, despite your best attempts to conform to their particular style of leadership.

Under circumstances like these, it may be best to develop a longer-term strategy. Certainly, you can confront a leader like this head-on and challenge their assessment of your capabilities. You can go to more senior leaders in the organization and complain. However, I've found it most productive to quietly lay out a different path and expend career currency planning the next professional move. If the current circumstances aren't working out, begin thinking about a move that removes you from the situation and allows you to realize, and be recognized for, your full potential.

The corollary to this advice is that even under the worst of circumstances, it is important to continue giving 100 percent to the job you are assigned and supporting your leader, even if that is a person whose leadership style you don't appreciate or who doesn't appreciate you. In the end, you'll be well served by taking the high road and playing the Long Game.

TAXES AND TARIFFS: UNETHICAL BOSSES

There's a critical caveat to playing the Long Game: you should never compromise your ethics for a substandard leader. If your boss's behavior goes beyond clashing with your style or adversely affecting your career plan to the point of being *wrong*, it is absolutely critical that you draw the line. Have the courage to report inappropriate behavior to the right person within your company. Don't allow yourself to go down with a sinking ship. There's a big difference between substandard leadership and lack of ethics or integrity. This is another element we'll talk more about in chapter 11.

CALCULATED EMOTION

Every rule has its exception, and the counsel against emotional displays has one too. There may be moments in your career when you need to emphasize your disappointment with a team's performance or an individual employee's inadequate effort. In such cases, *calculated emotion* can be a powerful tool—especially when you're someone who generally maintains your composure.

Instances of calculated emotion are thought of in advance and delivered within the bounds of professionalism. When executed properly, they can effectively illustrate that, for instance, an underperforming team must make changes.

I've never seen a better example of this than the time my boss was embroiled in difficult negotiations with another company. Negotiations that had dragged on for months. At the center of this was a crucial contract that both companies were working on, but the other side was being contentious and holding things up. So we had arranged a meeting between the two senior executives.

The meeting was a small luncheon, held in a small private room, with a small group of people in attendance. There were a couple of employees on either side with our bosses doing the talking. From the moment he walked in, my boss laid out his very reasonable plan and tried to explain—politely—different compromises that could resolve the disagreement between the two companies. The other gentleman, however, remained staunchly unreasonable. All we were getting out of the meeting was a decent lunch.

Then my boss—very uncharacteristically—raised his voice, smacked his fist on the table, and sharply stated that if we couldn't find a logical compromise, this discussion was over, and he was going to find another partner for the project.

Everything got quiet.

As quickly as my boss had changed his tone, the other individual changed his own. Now in a completely different negotiating posture, the other executive reached a handshake agreement with my boss by the end of the meeting, and we left knowing a problem that had loomed over the project for months was being resolved. As pleased as I felt with the outcome, I was still surprised at my boss's reaction during the meeting. As we drove back to our office, I said, "Wow, he must have really upset you, for you to have lost your temper that way. You seem like you were really upset with him."

I'll never forget how he looked at me and said, "That was planned from the moment we walked into the meeting."

My boss explained, "I knew this individual was likely to go down this path, and I knew at what point in the meeting I was going to get angry because I knew it would get his attention." He continued, "I hoped that he would respond in the right way, and he did."

In other words, my boss hadn't flown off the handle—screaming and speaking harshly because a stubborn individual had pushed him past the point of composure. He'd decided on a clear moment within the discussion when, if real progress had not been made, he would leverage an emotional effect in an effort to change the direction of the meeting.

In fact, he was the one who drove home the importance of this tactic for me, in no uncertain terms. "Never underestimate the value of calculated emotion," he said. "And never underestimate the negative effect of uncontrolled emotion in business."

When you are able to keep your negative emotions—or at least your outward reactions to them—in check and occasionally harness the power of calculated emotion, you will maximize your effectiveness in the workplace and earn the respect of your coworkers, team members, and business leadership. In turn, you'll position yourself well for future advancement opportunities, bolstering your career currency for the future.

CHAPTER 9

POSITIVE POLITICS

Being Political While Avoiding the Dark Side

I've debated long and hard about the inclusion of this chapter, and at the urging of a dear friend and trusted advisor, I've decided to make it part of the book. While I feel strongly that the foundation of any career is hard work, dedication, and results, I cannot deny the influence of politics—especially as one moves higher in an organization.

I've heard it said that "luck is the convergence of preparedness and opportunity." In rudimentary terms, I suppose one could consider preparedness to be a result of your dedication and performance, and opportunity to be driven—at least to some degree—by political factors that are cultivated through relationships. In order to reach the top, it's important to invest the lion's share of your career currency in dedicated performance that delivers results but also to spend a reasonable amount cultivating those relationships that will open doors for you.

Like many people, I don't like the notion of workplace politics. It has a very negative connotation in my mind. I have realized over time—and through conversations with coworkers, friends, and mentors—that there is a positive side to politics as well, though we may often use a completely different label for it. When objectively political measures are used for the good of your company, your superiors, your team, and yourself simultaneously, it's typically called *relationship building.*

At its best, on-the-job politics means lifting yourself up once in a while and getting beyond your immediate work group to get to know the people you work with—your peers and the people who lead larger portions of the organization—getting to know them and allowing them to get to know you. While it may seem this would be most important early in your career, it is essential to start this type of engagement early and continue it throughout your career.

To underscore this point, consider this example from my early days as a vice president in my company. I was working at the time under our company's CTO, leading corporate research and development programs. I had been in this position for about eighteen months and was starting to think about my next move. While I hoped that my job performance would position me well for my next role, I decided also to make time for career discussions with a number of senior leaders in the company, to ensure they were aware of my aspirations.

One such conversation was with our top human resources executive. When the meeting began and I started talking about my career goals and prior experiences, he stopped me almost immediately. It turned out that just that morning he had been in a meeting with senior leaders in another part of our company, and they were looking for someone with very similar credentials. Within twenty-four hours I was in discussions over the phone. Within a week I was on an airplane headed across the country for a job interview. Within sixty days I had begun a new assignment. All of this was because I had taken the time to share with others my goals and aspirations and to solicit new opportunities.

Part of getting a job done well and being a leader involves understanding not only your organization's objectives but other people's. When this is your focus, you strike a healthy give-and-take that helps move the company as a whole forward. That, in my mind, is the positive side of politics—trying to help others and from time to time asking them to help you. It's about relationships and trust.

On the other hand, there's a very negative side of workplace politics—the side people are more commonly referring to when they use the term. Those who engage in the negative side build alliances to move ahead at someone else's expense or to further an agenda that benefits them but not the company at large.

Fortunately, in my company I've seen very little of the negative side of politics, but you're going to encounter it to some degree, no matter how great your company and career field are. Because it can resonate in any organization, it's important to work out ways to stay above it, not to get involved, and not to fall victim to its pernicious undertow.

This becomes even more important when you occupy a leadership role. Those in positions of authority have the power to set clear expectations for employees that this kind of behavior will not be tolerated. The website *Management Study Guide* cites negative effects of workplace politics that include decreased productivity and concentration, demotivated employees, upticks in stress, and the wide dissemination of inaccurate information.

Beyond that, once you've embarked on this course, you'll find it to be time consuming and draining. When that sort of agenda has been set, people spend quite a bit of time thinking, "Let's see ... how do I undermine my colleague so that I look better in the boss's eyes? How do I take credit for something I didn't do?" The whole process is analogous to cheating on an exam. If an individual has cheated their way through two years of college and then suddenly decides to abandon the low road to actually start studying, they discover their academic muscles have atrophied after two years of nonuse. They're behind everyone else, and continuing to cheat seems like the easiest way to "keep up." Whether you're looking at someone else's test or swooping in to take credit for someone else's job performance, it becomes a surrogate for doing a good job and delivering consistent results.

Once, in the first five years of my career, I worked with a very high-performing group. We had a visionary leader who continuously pushed the boundaries of our charter to deliver greater value to our corporation. In general, we had a strong, focused, and collaborative team. As with any team, though, we had one or two members who relied more on backbiting and negative politics to preserve their position and get ahead. One such individual happened to sit in the cubicle next to me.

I was working quietly at my computer one day, when most of my colleagues were out of the office on business. I was deep in thought, doing research for a new project our boss had just launched. My colleague on the other side of the wall was talking on the phone— quietly but audibly—and all at once, the substance of his conversation brought every bit of my focus to what he had to say. He was speaking with a leader from a different part of the company. He was disparaging the new project I had just been assigned, along with our team and our boss. He was undermining our organization while trying to secure a promotional role with a new team.

I waited patiently for him to finish his call. I counted to ten and then walked around the corner and confronted him. As professionally as I could, I recounted what I had heard. He was clearly ashamed. We spoke for a while. In the end he apologized. When our boss returned, he apologized to him too. The transfer to the new department never materialized for him, and as far as I could tell, he didn't engage in that behavior again. I always wondered if he had learned his lesson, and I hoped that he had.

I find that all too often, though, people who engage in the underhanded tactics I've described here generally do not spend time learning how to do things *without* stepping on others. The easy way out becomes their go-to methodology, and they tend to keep it up until, eventually, someone sees behind the curtain.

And if engaging in negative politics ever does start to look alluring, it's helpful to keep in mind that someone does, eventually, see behind the curtain. Always. This happens not only because once you start, you tend to consistently act this way—making exposure only a matter of time—but also because the higher you rise in an organization, the harder it becomes to conceal your true colors. Someone who manages to climb all the way to the highest rung of the ladder by stepping on others and taking credit for their work doesn't suddenly expand their skill set once they're granted the hoped-for job. If they reach a senior leadership position and their main talent was using others, they simply won't be able to do the job they now have. They certainly won't last long in it.

You're better off behaving in a way that's inclusive and respectful of others from the very beginning. Err on the side of giving credit rather than taking it. Elevate yourself through your own hard work, dedication, and delivery of results for the greater good. This will serve you much better in the long run than trying to make it on someone else's steam.

TAXES AND TARIFFS: THE OTHER DARK SIDE

Early in my career, I was allergic to the notion of workplace politics, and therefore, I religiously focused on doing my job and delivering results. The results, I decided, would speak for themselves. Because of this, I really missed that there is a positive side to politics: taking the time to build relationships with those you work around (and wish to work around) can be not only auspicious for your career but also truly rewarding on a personal level.

Fortunately I had a mentor who pulled me aside and said, "You know, you can't always just do a good job and expect everybody to understand. You have aspirations, and you need to make them known to people who are in a position to help you. You do occasionally need to take the time to talk to other people—talk about what you're doing, and talk about your project. When you've been working on something and it produces good results, don't be afraid, every once in a while, to share the news—in a way that's humble and respectful, of course."

This was the first time I really understood this piece of the politics equation—that it could involve building healthy, positive relationships and making sure you and others in your organization benefit from mutual support. When it was put to me that way, I could at last understand it as a worthwhile undertaking.

I've covered the dark side of getting hooked into negative politics and sticking with it for years, but there's also a dark side of refusing to engage in positive politics. One day you might look back and realize you've been working your hardest for twenty-five years yet are stuck in the same old job because you didn't make your aspirations known to those who could have helped you achieve them. Someone who is more political may have been taking credit for your work, leveraging *your* career currency to get ahead.

The most important factor, relevant to both the positive and negative sides, is to make yourself *politically aware*. Doing so won't mean you automatically cross over to the "political dark side."

One of my better leaders, Joan, used to use that phrase. She would talk with me about what it really meant. I remember once in the course of a conversation about keeping your head down, doing a good job, and letting the results speak for themselves, she introduced me to another phrase that's stuck with me over the years: getting pecked to death by ducks.

Explaining the concept, Joan said that if somebody takes partial credit for one small task you've completed or fails to acknowledge one of your accomplishments, you might be inclined to let it roll off and just press forward. What's the big deal anyway?

"But you have to be careful, Jon," she told me, "that you don't wind up pecked to death by ducks. One dismissive comment about your job performance is no big deal—but think about a hundred of those." The same concept goes by other names as well, including death by a thousand paper cuts. Whatever you call it, the point is that slights against you, negative comments about your performance or teamwork, and minor taxes and fees levied against your career currency can add up fast and can prove to have an effect much more devastating than any of the individual incidents.

You need to be politically aware so you can recognize when there are people trying to quietly undermine you—and you need to have the courage to stand up for yourself if this happens. When you're politically aware, you're also more in tune with the many opportunities to be gained from the positive, relationship-building side of politics.

CHAPTER 10

BUILD A STRONG TEAM

Fill the Right Roles with the Right People

One of my favorite business books is *Good to Great*, by Jim Collins. This tried and true classic covers many leadership strategies that I have employed throughout my professional journey. One that is at the top of my list involves "Getting the Right People on the Bus." Collins argues that before you can move an organization toward a better future, you have to build the right team, and often this involves making some changes. I couldn't agree more.

Leadership is an exciting and rewarding undertaking, one that requires a very different skill set than being an individual contributor. Rather than succeeding or failing on the basis of your own personal effort and capabilities, you will succeed or fail based on the accomplishments of those who are part of your team. Your team's performance will be *the* primary measure of your professional achievements.

If at any point in your career, or any level of an organization, you fail to get the team-composition equation correct, you will pay a tax. Some career currency will be needlessly expended because you will get into some form of preventable trouble. A shoddily constructed team *will* encounter challenges that a team with the right balance wouldn't. And while assembling your team correctly is always important for this very reason, there's one time that it's especially critical: when you're given your first leadership assignment.

I'd like to emphasize that while first leadership assignments are of monumental importance, the advice I'm offering here applies to leadership at every stage of your career. You can be on your second, fifth, or fifteenth position as a leader and still benefit.

When you initially move from individual contributor to leader, everyone will be watching to see how you handle it.

When you're granted your first leadership assignment, it's your job to figure out how to best lead your team—and to figure it out quickly. If this critical first team of yours performs poorly, even for six months, that could equal a significant setback in your organization and thus lead to your being judged an incompetent leader. Once an impression like that is formed, it can take many, many years to recover and move on to other opportunities. That's why, while smart team building and leadership will always matter, these are especially important areas right out of the gate.

TAXES AND TARIFFS: EVERY EMPLOYEE IS DIFFERENT

All too often, I've seen high-potential employees who cannot make the leap from individual contributor to leader. These early-career leaders frequently drive their teams as they've always driven themselves—and why wouldn't they? It's what gotten them this far. But this is a terrible mistake, one that can cost you dearly in career currency. There are two pieces of advice I can offer those who find themselves in this scenario:

Listen: It's incredibly important to listen more than you speak. If you've risen quickly, chances are your people know more than you do about many things. Take the time to hear their perspectives and adjust your own course on the basis of their wisdom. Each employee has unique experiences and a unique point of view. This will yield two benefits. First, their input will likely help you make wiser decisions. Second, they will feel valued because their perspectives were heard and, in many cases, acted upon.

Win the popular vote: Rather than drive results through tasking and aggressive actioning of your staff, inspire them. Create a vision for your team that inspires them to follow you and deliver success for your organization. You must inspire them as a collective, but also as individuals. Over

> *time your team will come to respect you and feel a deep commitment to you as well as to the future of the organization. I've seen this work for organizations that have been on the rise, steady, or even on the decline. It's a hallmark of true leadership.*

I know exactly how hard it can be for early-career professionals to make the switch I'm talking about here, because it was hard for me.

Early in my career, I was driven and focused, which opened the door to a great deal of professional success. When I began leading teams, I surrounded myself with like-minded people to the extent possible, driving them all as I was accustomed to driving myself. I didn't truly grasp that my team comprised individuals with different styles, perspectives, and priorities. While my team respected and wanted to support me, I was eroding the morale of my team.

Fortunately, a senior leader in my organization pulled me aside and offered some counsel, which, also fortunately, I was mature enough to take onboard. From that point forward, I tried my best to look through the lenses of my team members rather than exclusively through my own. As a result of this approach, I was able to foster trust and open communication. In turn, this helped me smoothly transition into the role of a supportive leader who inspired his team to succeed—leveraging each employee's strengths and perspectives to the maximum extent.

Don't ever underestimate the power of empowering and supporting the people who work for you!

Of course, before you can focus on your leadership style, you have to have a team to lead. As a new leader, nine out of ten times you will inherit an existing team. This brings with it advantages and challenges. On one hand, an established team is generally able to keep routine business on track, allowing you an opportunity to come up to speed on your new role. On the other hand, an established team will have its own culture and method of doing things. This can be difficult when you're not adjusted to the culture and have different ideas about methodology.

The other downside of an established team is that you cannot initially choose the people who work for you. In order to build the right team, you will need to make incremental changes. All effective change takes time, and never is that as true as when you're talking about personnel.

However, there are some principles you should adhere to no matter what—whether you're the leader of an established team or building a group from scratch.

The attitude of your team members is infinitely more important than aptitude. One bad apple can disrupt the entire team and, in extreme cases, even lead to outright dysfunction. No depth of experience or talent is worth the price of bad behavior. Bad behavior of a team member can run the gamut from apathy to incompetence and all the way to actively undermining other members of the team.

Pessimism is another common team derailer. A team member who makes it clear they don't expect the team's efforts to go as planned, be appreciated, or matter at all can open a slow leak in the rest of the team's optimism. Someone who favors harsh versus constructive criticism and doesn't offer support for good ideas can contribute to an atmosphere in which team members are reluctant to share even their brightest thoughts.

These are only a few of the bad-attitude manifestations that can either spread throughout the team or undermine other team members' productive efforts. When you look out for these behaviors and make it clear you won't tolerate them, you're pledging your support for those who do things the right way.

As leaders, we can sometimes be slow to take action when we see bad behavior. After all, addressing these personnel issues involves confronting the offending individuals. It can be uncomfortable and may lead to someone losing their job. But if the bad actors are not able to correct their behavior, it is imperative that you act decisively and make personnel changes to remove these individuals from the team.

Another common mistake leaders make is to surround themselves with people just like them. Unfortunately, as driven professionals entering leadership, many fall into this trap. It is important to seek out people with different backgrounds, perspectives, and styles. When combined with a culture that invites healthy debate, this heterogeneous team model will always limit blind spots and produce superior results.

In its "Small Business" section, the *Houston Chronicle* emphasizes one of several benefits of cultivating a company or team that's diverse not only in terms of demographic features but in ideas and temperaments. This makes it easier to achieve team balance. "Employees who are quiet and introverted often help to stabilize things at work, but workers who are risk takers can provide the spark necessary to try new things, develop bolder ideas, and suggest improvements that can boost efficiency." A varied team has positive implications for workplace morale, decision-making, and overall efficiency.

The culture of a team or organization is the most important contributor to long-term success. As you build your team, it is important that everyone buy in to a common view of culture and work environment—and that everyone align around a common set of results for the team. In fact, according to Deloitte, "94% of executives and

88% of employees believe a distinct workplace culture is important to business success."

If you are able to adhere to these principles, you'll be ready to select, develop, and (as necessary) change members of your team. While every team's needs are different, there are a number of roles that tend to prove their worth across the spectrum when it comes to long-term success. While the purpose and objectives of teams will differ vastly within and across companies, leaders are well advised to find the right people to fill the following roles:

1. Trusted Advisor: This is the person in whom you will confide most everything. It must be a person you trust implicitly and who is willing to tell you the things you don't want to hear—as well as someone who tends to see your blind spots.

2. Devil's Advocate: Not nearly as sinister as the title implies, this person is great when it comes to considering alternative viewpoints. If you watch carefully, you may realize you have someone on your existing team who's naturally inclined to take this role. Is there someone who, in most meetings, uses compare-and-contrast language? Someone who makes a valid point and then says, "Though, on the other hand ..."? If there's not that one well-suited individual, you may need to assign different team members to the role on a case-by-case basis.

3. Domain Expert: If you are moving rapidly in your career, chances are you will be leading teams who know more about the domain in which the team works than you do. If this is the case, identify someone you can trust who has deep knowledge of the domain and lean on that person for

counsel. It's far wiser to acknowledge the areas where your knowledge isn't deep and to lean on someone else than to fake it for all the world to see.

I've had the good fortune to have moved many times in my career and worked in different parts of my company. And that's great from a general management perspective, but it's difficult to step into a new role that has a lot of highly technical projects active when you walk in the door. One of the first things I do in these situations is seek out one or two people who have a deep understanding of the particular customer set that we work with, the particular products we offer in this area, and the challenges that our company as well as our customer base faces. For someone who's accustomed to moving across different disciplines within a company, it's critically important to find these individuals—the domain experts.

4. Newcomer: Once you've been with your team awhile, it will benefit you to bring on someone with a fresh perspective—it will benefit everyone. When that new person joins, take the time to seek out their perspective. They will see things others don't because they have been part of the team for so long.

5. Steady Performer: As much as I have always tried to recruit high performers to my teams, over time I've come to realize that not everyone seeks the path to the top. Many competent individuals in the workforce find their niche in a company and then want only to deliver value in that particular role. A healthy team comprises not just high flyers but also steady performers with tenure in the business,

those who come to work every day and make a meaningful contribution.

6. High Potential: It's also important to recruit employees with potential. Seek out those who are on the rise, and stretch them by matching them to ambitious roles. I've found these individuals challenge the status quo and are driven to make vast contributions as they strive to move ahead. The caution is to ensure that you keep them challenged and help them chart a course to their next role—while still placing the needs of the business above their own personal interests.

7. Cheerleader: One of the easier-to-recognize valuable players is the cheerleader. The person who energizes the whole team. If you're lucky enough to be that person—great! If you're somewhat introverted, like me, it's okay to look to a member of your team to infuse the team with some excitement and charisma.

8. Analyst: Every team needs a deep thinker. If that's not you, look for the person who's always quietly parsing the data that sits below the surface within your organization. Facts, figures, financials, technical data. Someone who keeps an eye on the numbers and tracks important trends can help the team remain objective and focused on demonstrable results.

9. Strategist: Finally, you need to ensure you have someone on your team thinking lofty thoughts about the future. Ideally, the leader of the team (you!) is this person, but it doesn't have to be if that isn't your orientation. However, it's imperative that someone from your team is always looking over the horizon. Whether it's months, years, or even a

decade ahead, it's critical that you plan for the future. The higher you go in an organization, the longer your time horizon. Keep cultivating and leveraging this critical skill.

These roles aren't always discrete—sometimes you can find one inside the other. You might be able to cultivate an individual who's already on your team and reposition them to be much more effective, taking on two, three, or even four of these roles.

Take Sharon, for example, a trusted advisor who I worked with in a previous position. While all good leaders draw on multiple advisors with diverse perspectives, I looked often to Sharon for her particularly keen insights. I came to realize that one reason I relied so heavily on her advice was that she was also an exceptionally seasoned devil's advocate. You may not necessarily think of those two going together, but sometimes they can, and that contrarian point of view is a critical ingredient of well-balanced decision-making.

Over time I worked to unpack and understand Sharon's strengths and talents, and I became convinced that she could add even more value to the team if her role were expanded. I asked her to take on a new position that would allow her to work in several areas of the business where she was a domain expert, and I also asked her to work closely with me on our annual strategy refresh for the business. As it turns out, Sharon was also a brilliant strategic thinker. By my account she was able to effectively play four or more of the roles I described earlier in this chapter, depending on the circumstance.

While every member of every team may not be as versatile as Sharon, I strongly encourage spending ample time thinking about the experience and talents of every team member. Look at each of them not only through the lens of the work they are doing today but also through the lens of their full potential. Even a subtle shift of responsibilities or job assignments might unlock a wealth of additional value for your team and for your career currency as a leader.

This chapter has taken you through what to do when you're the leader. Next we'll look at a scenario that can be even hairier: what to do when someone else is the leader ... and they're bad at it.

CHAPTER 11

THE TRUTH ABOUT BAD BOSSES

The Importance of Working for Good People

Of all the lessons I've learned in my career, the one I'm about to share is one of the simplest but also one of the most profound.

I've been fortunate—over the years and across dozens of roles—to work for some of the best professionals you could hope for. The few occasions when I haven't been so fortunate, however, really stand out—occasions when I worked for individuals who simply made poor leaders or were even unethical. Luckily, I experienced the latter only once.

Through my encounters with these leaders, it has been made unmistakably clear to me that your boss can make or break your success in a job. A series of good or bad bosses can make or break your career. Spending too much time with a consistently bad leader is the Ponzi scheme of bad career currency investments. If you find yourself in such a situation, you may need a little time to maneuver, but it's best to look for the earliest possible exit strategy.

In the early years of my career, I was very fortunate to work for great leaders. Empowering and nurturing, they always did their best to help me get ahead. I encountered my first poor leader when I had been with the business for about six years. In addition to being dishonest with me about advocating for me and my career, he was dishonest with customers and would cross moral lines to get ahead. And thanks to his reputation for being very temperamental, everyone in our office walked on eggshells around him.

Ethically, this was a complicated scenario. I was a relatively new leader who already had a lot invested in the job—including the fact that I had relocated for it. I was still learning the ropes when I was placed into this person's orbit. Facets of his personality became apparent to me immediately: he was volatile, he was incredibly difficult to work with, and he was feared. It was only later, though, that I learned of the ethical violations. After the fact, when he'd been removed from his post, I heard that he hadn't been following company procedures and had done some things that were certainly on the edge, if not outright wrong.

Within a few months, I had a full picture of the person I was working for, but unfortunately that didn't make my own path forward clear. It called for delicate handling, as I wanted to stay with my company but at the same time knew I needed to move to a different organization. I was still weighing my options when fate smiled on me and my boss's superiors took note of his bad behavior. A few months later, I was moved to a different part of the organization, and my boss's responsibilities were modified based on his performance and behavior. While he survived with the company a bit longer, in the end he was asked to leave.

While not a pleasant experience for me, this certainly taught me a few lessons about how damaging bad behavior can be with any company and how demoralizing, and career limiting, it can be to work for a bad boss. In this particular case, luck intervened and gave me an out. But I've often reflected on the bind I was in while working for him, and I've asked myself what I would do differently if I could—and what I would advise others to do if they're tethered to a boss like him.

At that stage in my career—and having just moved for this job—I was trying to find a way to make it work. If I had to do it over again, with the years of wisdom under my belt, I might have gone and spoken to his boss and tried to have a conversation about the behaviors I was witnessing, or I might have tried to talk to some of my colleagues and see maybe if we could do that together, with a goal of getting him some coaching or counseling. Without a doubt, he was smart. He knew the business well. He just didn't have the right temperament and the right values to lead a team.

In certain rare cases, going over your boss's head, reporting their behavior to *their* boss, may be your only useful course of action. Naturally, this is considered a fairly drastic step, and you should take the time to thoroughly evaluate the situation before taking action. While you should never have to feel guilty or self-conscious for reporting behavior that violates your values, or the company's, you need to make sure this step is warranted.

Here's what I mean by that: on one hand, there's having a bad boss; on the other, there's having bad chemistry. If you're not certain which it is, give it some time. Carefully observe the patterns in your boss's behavior. If your knee-jerk reaction is to label something your boss has done as bad, try looking at the action as objectively as possible. Ask yourself whether, if a leader with whom you have much better rapport did the same thing, you would still be convinced it was wrong. If you're still convinced, take the time to carefully seek out a trusted confidante or two in the organization and gather additional perspective on your concerns.

While these situations need to be evaluated carefully, it shouldn't take long to draw your conclusions. If you're focused and forward thinking enough to have risen quickly in your career, you can probably work out whether your boss's personality and style simply clash with your own or whether your boss is acting in a way that could do irreparable harm to your career, to the company's reputation, and even to your customers.

The right course of action is quite different depending on whether you're looking at bad chemistry or a bad boss—and it can be a complicated equation. When there's bad chemistry, you can often navigate through the situation over a period of time. You can quietly look for another opportunity to move along and leave this challenging leader behind as you press forward.

But if you're working for someone who's abusive or otherwise crosses ethical lines, it may prove harmful for you to restrict your efforts to quietly looking for an opportunity to get away. At a certain point, you really have an obligation to speak up.

I'd like to briefly call attention back to the planning I outlined previously in this book—the planning involved in mapping out your career in accordance with your true career priorities, interests, and capabilities. When you get to the point in your planning of deciding what qualities that specific organization you work for should have, there's an important one you may want to consider: whether there's infrastructure in place—a clear-cut process, a policy—for reporting inappropriate behavior without fear of retaliation.

This is something that's taken very, very seriously at Lockheed Martin. Our company maintains a zero-tolerance policy for retaliation. There's a confidential, independent reporting chain for ethical issues. In fact, we have an ethics hotline, which anybody in the entire company can anonymously contact. Employees who experience anything from a hostile work environment to sexual harassment to intimidation to openly illegal behavior have a way to report it without fearing that they will miss out on future opportunities or even lose their current job because they've spoken up. And I can attest that all matters reported are taken seriously and investigated.

I'm proud to work for a company that has laid out a clear, structured path for doing the right thing. Because of this, I can feel confident that improper conduct will be weeded out of the ranks—and that those who tend to engage in it will be discouraged from ever entering an environment of such transparency. If you have the foresight to look for a similar system in companies you consider working for, that takes claims seriously and is backed by an integrated system of company values, your path forward when it comes to *truly* bad bosses will be less confusing.

But if you work in an organization where there's not a cut-and-dried method for reporting these matters with impunity—and if you have determined that your boss is genuinely acting unethically rather than it being a matter of bad chemistry—a large question looms. If, in your judgment, reporting the behavior is not going to end well, you should probably look for an opportunity to leave the organization. At that point, it comes down to your livelihood. You simply have to balance your financial needs with your need to get out at the earliest opportunity.

TAXES AND TARIFFS: DON'T FORGET CHAPTER 8

I have had a couple of bad bosses over the years. These were frustrating situations, and in general I handled them as well as I believe could have been expected. There was one exception, however. I had a boss who was fond of public criticism. He would usually engage professionally with team members in one-on-one settings, but in group meetings he would frequently attack members of our team, sometimes even questioning their integrity.

On one such occasion, I was the target of his criticism. Having observed and occasionally endured this behavior in the past, I reached a breaking point. I pushed back—hard. I yelled at my boss. In public. And yes, if I'm honest, it felt good—in the moment. And not being accustomed to this sort of response, my boss surprisingly apologized in front of the group.

You might read this example and conclude I had taken the right action. After all, my boss apologized and admitted he was out of line. But my behavior was out of line also. I had lost my cool and stooped to the same level of behavior he was exhibiting. All of my colleagues witnessed that, and I am sure it wasn't forgotten.

While I was fortunate that this scenario ended the way it did, the situation could have escalated into a shouting match or, worse, created a permanent fracture with my leader. What I might have done instead was take the moment in stride and planned an opportunity to address my boss's behavior with him in private. It probably would have led to the same outcome, and I wouldn't have left a group of my coworkers with the memory of my emotional outburst.

The lesson here is not to let a bad boss get so far under your skin that you blow more career currency by stooping to their level. Always remember chapter 8, and plan your moments to push back or take other action.

I know I have spent much of this chapter focusing on bad bosses and what to do about them, but I'd like to end by focusing on the good ones. Because the good ones are worth their weight in gold.

One such boss was Janette, a woman I worked for a little more than ten years ago. I had held a series of assignments wherein I handled strategic projects focused on expansion of our business. I'd also found success, and visibility, in working on proposals for new contracts. Around this time, I had a few career discussions with mentors that all contained a similar theme: "Boy, it would be good for you to remove all doubt about your ability to actually run a big, complicated piece of our business. You've done a great job with the strategy. You've done a great job with bringing in new work. How would you do with something really big, really hard, and really complicated?"

After hearing this same message from a few different people I trusted, I had a conversation in passing with my boss's boss, our division president. Well, soon after, she called me up and said, "You know the program we won about nine months ago that so far hasn't been doing well? I've decided it would be good for you to take it over. You start Monday morning"—today was Wednesday—"and it's going to involve daily meetings with my boss at seven thirty in the morning to provide status updates, as this is a troubled project."

It was the hardest assignment I've ever taken on professionally. For long stretches of it, I was working until late at night, often seven days a week. But within eighteen months, I had led the turnaround of the project and helped our customer realize success.

This ended up being a milestone in my career and a leadership experience that would inspire the confidence in my own abilities that I needed. It took an excellent boss to take our passing discussion seriously, to keep her eyes open for an experience that matched my abilities as well as the areas where I needed to grow, and to place so much trust in me.

At several points in this book, I've mentioned Terry, my best mentor ever. But before he became my mentor, he was my boss. Terry originally hired me to be what's called a technical assistant. In our company, technical assistants differ from administrative assistants. They travel with you, put together presentation materials, send weekly reports to the corporate office, and complete other pivotal tasks—almost like a chief of staff.

A technical assistant job usually lasts somewhere between a year and eighteen months. So I took the position as Terry's technical assistant and relocated to Washington, DC, in August of 2001.

A month later, I was at the dentist when an airplane flew into the World Trade Center.

Now, our division at Lockheed Martin happened to have this sleepy little side business doing some airport security work. All of a sudden, we got a call from the corporate office when our government established the new Transportation Security Administration, what we know now as the TSA. Our sleepy little side business was about to be overwhelmed with critical national security work. All hands were on deck, and I immediately jumped into the efforts supporting this new agency, trying to assist however I could. I was energized and excited when contracts started coming in to secure our nation's airports.

I had served as Terry's technical assistant for only seven months. He had spent money and time to relocate me to DC and train me to do the job. But he could see how excited I was about the TSA mission. He said, "You know what, Jon? There are great career opportunities here. I hate for you to miss them. I want you to go pursue this. I'll find somebody else to come and do this job."

And so he released me. He gave up an assistant he had just finished training because he saw that I was going to have opportunities and didn't want me to miss them. These were opportunities to serve our country during a time of crisis and to take an important career step into the leadership ranks. Terry didn't make it about him. It was all about me and where I would be most valued—my own growth, our company's and our nation's needs, and also my career currency.

"Don't worry," he told me, "and don't look back. Go do good things, and make me proud." That's the kind of leader he was. He modeled what true leadership is, and his example and insights are still with me today.

CONCLUSION

A CALL TO ACTION

GIVE 110 PERCENT—EVERY DAY

There is no substitute for giving all of yourself every day at the office. This doesn't just mean your technical skills and abilities. It also applies to the attitude and energy you bring to the work—even if the role you're in at the moment isn't exactly your dream job!

Are you expressing interest? Showing your willingness to raise your hand and take on additional assignments?

Make sure you're all in—every day. You are creating a personal brand that will follow you throughout your career (just like those old pictures you posted on Facebook or Instagram when you were in college). Your résumé will live in the shadow of the brand you bring to life. You owe it to yourself to make it the gold standard.

SIT WITH STRANGERS

As humans, we tend to gravitate toward the familiar. How often do you enter a room at a social function and scope out the room to find someone you already know? Or grab lunch with your office mate whom you spend all your time with?

For focused professionals who spend our days and weeks engaging with a multitude of colleagues and customers, the idea of engaging with one more person we don't know can at times feel downright exhausting. Still, the idea of connecting with others is fundamental to business success.

Are you sitting with *coworkers* who are strangers? Studies have shown that the most diverse organizations are the ones that perform best—but we can fully capture that value only when we engage with that diverse population in an inclusive way.

Are you partnering across your enterprise to deliver maximum value for your customers? Do you even know what you don't know about other parts of your organization, or could sitting with a stranger help open your eyes?

Are you sitting with *customers* who are strangers? Do you have one point of contact whom you always deal with? Or might there be a rising star in the organization who will be a key decision maker soon?

Does sitting with strangers unlock the potential to be not only better at business but better as people? Try sitting with strangers. It may be uncomfortable at first, but I don't think you'll regret it.

DON'T FORGET TO SPEND SOME CURRENCY ON YOURSELF

There are reasons it's important to spend our career currency wisely, reasons that have nothing to do with work itself. While time is your career currency, it is also your life currency. It's true that you need to be mindful of your expenditures, taxes, and overall valuation when it comes to the currency of your career. It is also important to ensure that you consider the balance of your life currency and how that is spent.

Knowing how to wisely manage your career is one of many tools you'll use over the years in the name of living a balanced, happy life—one in which you reach for both your professional and personal goals. The advice offered in this book is a tool, a resource—something you can use to realize your professional goals. It shouldn't become an obsession. It needn't come at the expense of your family and friends or your time for yourself.

Before I close, I'd like to share one more story about Terry.

One day, as we talked he drew three intersecting circles in a triangular pattern on a whiteboard. In the first circle, he wrote *career*. In the second, he wrote *family*. And in the last circle, he wrote *self*. These three circles intersected not only visibly but also logically for me. I could see how they were each distinct but also intertwined.

He told me, "As much as it's important to focus on your career, if these three circles fall out of balance, *you're* going to fall out of balance. So make sure you're always thinking about all three and giving each the attention it needs."

As much as we've focused on the *career* circle in this book, I want to leave you with the parting advice to keep all three in balance. After all, the advice comes straight from Terry.

BIBLIOGRAPHY

"A Day in the Life of a Computer Engineer/Systems Analyst." *The Princeton Review*. https://www.princetonreview.com/careers/42/ computer-engineer-systems-analyst.

Alamispark. "How Well Are You Investing Your Time?" Youtube. https://www.youtube.com/watch?v=nH5K0yo-o1A.

Andersen, Erika. "Admitting You Don't Know, When You're the CEO." *Harvard Business Review*. August 17, 2015. https://hbr. org/2015/08/admitting-you-dont-know-when-youre-the-ceo.

"Best Careers for INTJ Personalities." Indeed career guide. Accessed October 18, 2018. https://www.indeed.com/career-advice/ finding-a-job/best-careers-for-intj-personalities.

Blake, Jenny. *Pivot*.

"Career Progression Opportunities in Retail Banking." All About Finance Careers. https://www.allaboutfinancecareers.co.uk/ industry/retail-banking/career-progression-opportunities- in-retail-banking.

Collins, Jim. *Good to Great.*

"Core Beliefs and Culture: Chairman's Survey Findings." Deloitte
    Development LLC. 2012. https://www2.deloitte.com/content/
    dam/Deloitte/global/Documents/About-Deloitte/gx-core-
    beliefs-and-culture.pdf.

Covey, Stephen. *7 Habits of Highly Effective People.*

"Effect of Politics on Organization and Employees." Management
    Study Guide. https://www.managementstudyguide.com/effect-
    of-politics.htm.

"Fast Facts." National Center for Educational Statistics. Accessed
    October 17, 2018. https://nces.ed.gov/fastfacts/display.
    asp?id=372.

Gilbert, Mandy. "Why Saying 'I Don't Know' Is a Sign of a Strong
    Leader." Inc.com. June 29, 2017. https://www.inc.com/mandy-
    gilbert/bif-you-always-claim-to-know-the-answer-you-migh.
    html.

Gladwell, Malcolm. *Outliers.*

Gupta, Guarav. "The Power of Saying 'I Don't Know'."
    Forbes. November 29, 2016. https://www.forbes.com/
    sites/johnkotter/2016/11/29/the-power-of-saying-i-dont-
    know/#6d3f7d411858; Kristi Hedges. "Six Ways to Con-
    fidently Say 'I Don't Know'." *Forbes*. May 4, 2015. https://
    www.forbes.com/sites/work-in-progress/2015/05/04/
    six-ways-to-confidently-say-i-dont-know/#246f7c7a2c66.

Lebowitz, Shana. "Adopting This Surprising Habit of Highly
    Intelligent People Can Make You Look Smarter at Work."

Business Insider. July 7, 2015. https://www.businessinsider.com/
saying-i-dont-know-makes-you-look-smart-2015-7.

Lee, Mike. "[8.4] The Great Crane Robbery." KACL780.NET.
2000. http://www.kacl780.net/frasier/transcripts/season_8/
episode_4/the_great_crane_robbery.html; "The Great Crane
Robbery." IMDb. https://www.imdb.com/title/tt0582532.

Marcec, Dan. "CEO Tenure Rates." Harvard Law School
Forum. February 12, 2018. https://corpgov.law.harvard.
edu/2018/02/12/ceo-tenure-rates/.

"Our Framework." 16Personalities. Accessed October 18, 2018.
https://www.16personalities.com/articles/our-theory.

Phillips, Ian. "Here's the Grueling and Intense Process It Takes to
Put Together One Episode of 'SNL.'" *Business Insider*. July 8,
2015. https://www.businessinsider.com/saturday-night-live-
how-an-episode-is-put-together-2015-7; Larry Getlen. "A Week
Behind the Scenes at 'SNL.'" *New York Post*. February 14, 2015.
https://nypost.com/2015/02/14/a-week-behind-the-scenes-at-
saturday-night-live.

Pofeldt, Elaine. "Are We Ready for a Workforce That Is 50%
Freelance?" *Forbes*. October 17, 2017. https://www.forbes.com/
sites/elainepofeldt/2017/10/17/are-we-ready-for-a-workforce-
that-is-50-freelance/#22b68a413f82.

Quain, Sampson. "What Are the Benefits of Having Different Personalities & Temperaments in the Workplace?" Chron. October
25, 2018. https://smallbusiness.chron.com/benefits-having-
different-personalities-temperaments-workplace-34480.html.

Saujani, Reshma. "Teach Girls Bravery, Not Perfection." Medium. March 8, 2016, https://medium.com/girls-who-code/teach-girls-bravery-not-perfection-257691d13476.

Taylor, Sequoia. "How to Build a Career in Venture Capital." Jopwell. April 7, 2017. https://www.glassdoor.com/blog/venture-capital/.

"Top Executives: Job Outlook." Bureau of Labor Statistics. Last modified April 13, 2018. https://www.bls.gov/ooh/management/top-executives.htm#tab-6.

"What is the SDS?" Self-Directed Search. Accessed October 19, 2018. http://www.self-directed-search.com/What-is-it.

Zipkin, Nina. "18 Ways to Calm Down When You're Stressed." *Entrepreneur*. April 9, 2018. https://www.entrepreneur.com/slideshow/302237.

CPSIA information can be obtained
at www.ICGtesting.com
Printed in the USA
BVHW011102211019
561643BV00010B/98/P